HOW TO BECOME A PUBLISHED WRITER: (ADVICE TO AUTHORS BOOK 2)

& LIVE TO TELL THE TALE
HELEN COX

Helen Cox Books

Copyright © 2020 by Helen Cox.

Published in the United Kingdom by Helen Cox Books.

No part of this book may be used or reproduced in any manner whatsoever without written permission except in the case of brief quotations embodied in critical articles or reviews. For further information, visit helencoxbooks.com. Copyright © 2020 by Helen Cox.

This book is written in British English.

Ebook ISBN: 978-1-8380221-3-6

Paperback ISBN: 978-1-8380221-4-3

Hardback ISBN: 978-1-8380221-5-0

How to Become a Published Writer

& Live to Tell the Tale

Helen Cox

Contents

Reviews of the Advice to Authors Series	I
1. INTRODUCTION	1
2. CHAPTER 1: PERMISSION	3
3. CHAPTER 2: THE FULL-TIME WRITER	10
4. CHAPTER 3: PURPOSE	19
5. CHAPTER 4: COURAGE	24
6. CHAPTER 5: TOUGH LOVE	30
7. CHAPTER 6: ORIGINALITY	38
8. CHAPTER 7: BLOCKS	43
9. CHAPTER 8: GOALS	50
10. CHAPTER 9: COMPARISONITIS	56
11. CHAPTER 10: TAKING FEEDBACK	59
12. CHAPTER 11: BEWARE ABSOLUTES	67

13. CHAPTER 12: THE END?	72
14. CHAPTER 13: HANDLING REJECTION	78
15. CHAPTER 14: COMPLETION	87
16. CHAPTER 15: HANDLING BAD REVIEWS	91
17. CHAPTER 16: MOVING ON	98
18. GOOD WRITING DAY PROMPTS	102
19. ACKNOWLEDGEMENTS	105
More Free Resources	106
About the Author	107
Also By Helen Cox	108

REVIEWS OF THE ADVICE TO AUTHORS SERIES

'Written from the heart with real experience and wisdom.'

'The author digs deep into her wealth of experience.'

'It's like having your own personal friendly mentor.'

'If you're looking to take your writing seriously, Helen's books will help you become a better writer!'

INTRODUCTION

The question of how to become a published writer is such a simple one on the face of it, right? The answer is surely, and reasonably, to write stories, poems or scripts aplenty until one of them eventually gets picked up by a commissioning editor or producer.

It is really that straightforward when it comes down to it.

And yet, every year, I cross paths with hundreds of creative writing students and authors alike who are frustrated, blocked and despairing with the process. They've suffered the affront of rejection too many times, they tell me. Or they've been unceremoniously dropped by their publisher. Or they just can't translate the vision in their head into words. This book is for those people. They are many and I have been one of them. Given that I plan to write until my dying day (even if by that point I'm not writing anything more intellectually taxing than Gilmore Girls fan-fiction), there is a good chance I shall be one of them again. For the process of writing is so acutely entwined with our self-esteem, our sense of identity and our purpose in this world that it is often difficult to differentiate between our writing and us. This, in turn, leads to a slow drowning in an ocean of subconscious lies we tell ourselves about our craft and our ability to contribute meaningfully to the world.

What follows are a series of strategies that will, I hope, offer you a way forward when dealing with some of the more demoralizing aspects of becoming a published writer. When I was five, my school teacher wrote on my report card that I had a 'wisdom beyond my years' and I am the holder of a 2.1 Bsc in Psychology from the University of Teesside. The second-most prestigious award a university student can be granted in a UK Higher Education institution. So I think we can all agree that I am qualified to advise on complicated creative and emotional issues. I think we can also all agree that I have a rather silly sense of humour and that you are likely to see more of it throughout these pages.

As you read, please take heart in this: if you are feeling lost on your writing journey, you are not alone. Your feelings are both legitimate and worthy of exploration. And lastly, you are here by choice. It may not always feel like it. Many writers feel as though they must write to breathe. But truly, you are under no obligation. So far as I know, the universe will not implode if you don't up your word count today. So if dedication to the craft poses risk to your wellbeing you have the freedom to step away, self-care and get some space from the blankness of the page. Staring into nothingness for hours on end is bound to have an impact on a person. So, give yourself a break and put your health before the creation of the next Booker Prize-winning novel. Acknowledge that writing well is a jolly good achievement, but it doesn't have to be everything.

CHAPTER 1: PERMISSION

"The question isn't who is going to let me; it's who is going to stop me." – **Ayn Rand**

Astronomical theory sets out an argument for many possible parallel universes, and many possible alternate planet earths. These parallel planet earths are not forced to follow the same laws of physics as ours does. There, it might be possible for human beings to walk up walls without Gene Kelly's expertise in dance, or float up to the moon whenever they fancy just by clicking their fingers. With infinite possibilities, it seems likely that a parallel universe could exist in which there are no traditional publishers. In which anyone who creates art, literature, music, dance or drama does so on their own steam without the need to receive validation, acceptance or legitimacy from traditional gatekeepers of the craft.

In the post-internet universe, there are ways of transporting yourself to such a world and those methods of teleportation will be explored in this book. In fulfilling the promise made in the title of this volume, in exploring strategies, pathways and psychological constructs that support you in becoming a published writer, I will not rule out any possibilities. Why would I do that when we writers need all the help we can find? I will thus discuss the role independent publishing can play in enriching your literary career in addition to being published the 'good old-fashioned' way.

Right now however, it's important we get something very basic and very primal out of the way. Because we don't live in that parallel universe where traditional publishers don't exist. We have all grown up under the doctrine of traditional publishers. As such, we are expected to submit our creative work for approval to editors, agents and publishers. We've learnt terms like 'slush pile' – an abhorrent way to describe the creative attempts of fellow human beings. We are one of the many million 'unsolicited'. And because many of us, myself included, will spend or have spent several years, maybe even a decade or two, toiling away as the unsolicited, unpublished writer it is vital to get this following point straight: **you don't need permission to create.**

If you wait around for someone to approve a poem or a story or a novel or a script, you could waste a lot of precious craft time or worse, get so hung up on whether someone will accept your work that you never put it out into the world at all. Newsflash: writing is not the kind of craft in which you, the writer, wait for your ship to sail into port. It is the kind of craft where you swim out into frightening depths in order to meet that ship before it sails by.

Waiting for another person's approval is a mistake I made even after I'd had several books published. My first two novels were set in New York City and were part of a series. The publisher had previously expressed fervent interest in publishing more of these books, so I thought there was a strong likelihood that my contract with the publisher would be renewed. Unfortunately, those books didn't sell. Not in any great numbers. A couple of thousand copies, but no more than that.

There was nothing wrong with the stories, by the way. The reviews from those who did pick them up were lovely, at times even flattering. But the covers for the books weren't a fit for the market at the time. And though the publisher put together an excellent marketing plan, it wasn't executed. Consequently, very few people even knew this product was available. The magic number of books weren't sold and my contract was not renewed.

At the risk of in any way diminishing your enthusiasm for having your book published, I have to be honest and tell you that this is a familiar story in the world of publishing. It happens to authors all the time. The good news is: it needn't be the end of the world.

In my case, however, I stalled in my writing. I had waited around for the publisher for a few months while they made their decision. I hadn't thought about what else I might write next, believing that was contingent on my publisher. So, when my contract wasn't renewed, I floundered. I was unsure of what to write next and noted, with frustration, that I could have been three months into my next project had I not waited for somebody else to give the green light on my next creation. Obviously, I shouldn't have started the next book in that particular series without a contract, but I could have been writing something else entirely. Developing my craft and possibly even writing something that my agent could sell at a later date.

Gratefully, not all was lost just because I'd inadvertently sailed into uncertain waters. During the process of getting my first two novels published, I had acquired the aforementioned agent. And not just any agent: the World's Loveliest Agent. The kind of agent who doesn't drop you just because your publisher decides not to renew your contract. If you're interested in having your books traditionally published, I recommend doing all you can to find a really excellent agent. I offer more information on how you might go about that in my book *How & When to Sign a Book Deal*.

It was my agent, Joanna Swainson, who steered my ship back into calm seas by suggesting I write a series of mystery stories set in York. As soon as she proposed this, sparks of inspiration began to fly and eighteen months later I had a draft of a third novel that was ready to send out to publishers.

You may notice my writing career wasn't over just because a publisher chose not to renew my contract for reasons I had little control over. A new publisher picked up my next series of books, but even if they hadn't my career as a writer still wouldn't have been over. I could have done one of several things with those books that didn't even involve a publisher. I could have published a chapter every day to my website for the sheer enjoyment of sharing mystery stories, perhaps asking people to make an online donation to read each chapter. Or to vote on where the story should go next and who the killer should be. I could have published the books myself using one of several internet services. I could have entered the manuscript into competitions hoping to be short-listed or even win a prize that might make traditional publishers think twice about both me and my manuscript. I could have put it in a drawer and started writing a new book, keeping the faith that at some point a publisher would accept another book from me, maybe a bestseller, and then ask: 'you don't have anything sitting in a drawer do you?' It might surprise you how often this question is asked of established authors with a proven readership.

Not only was my writing career not over because a publisher dropped me, it wouldn't have been over even if no other publisher had accepted a manuscript from me for as long as I lived. While holding true to the focus of this book of becoming a published writer, it is important to underline here that writers and published writers are two different animals. Most of us are writers first, long before we are published writers. Never becoming a published writer would not stop us from being writers so long as we keep writing on a regular basis.

The requirement for being a writer is simply that you write. You don't need somebody else's approval or opinion to achieve this. You (hopefully) have the instruments to write at any time of your choosing. And you also hopefully understand that you can write whatever you so wish without the need to worry about market trends and whether in the long-term what you write might turn into something publishable. So whatever advice and guidance follows in the remaining pages of this book always remember this: writing is a craft, an art, and above all else it is wise to find some pleasure in it. Rather than seeking permission, I highly recommend you seek joy. This is not just because I want the best for you, fellow human being. Joy actually facilitates getting published. Yes, joy can be a business strategy of sorts.

Hear me out.

Are you more or less likely to give your time to a project that makes you happy? That feels more like having fun than knuckling down to work? I can't answer for you, but I know how I feel about this. If something feels like a chore, it will go straight to the bottom of my to-do list. And if my heart isn't in a piece of writing it definitely feels more like a chore than anything else.

Not only will seeking joy instead of permission raise your productivity levels, in my experience it's also more likely to entice and engage readers.

If writing does not bring you joy, any potential readers, everyone from editors and agents to bookworms, are likely to feel that lacklustre undercurrent in your work from page one. I don't know how they do it exactly. But I suppose those of us familiar with superhero narrative might call it a Spidey-sense. I have this Spidey-sense too when I'm reading a book and I can just feel that the writer is painting by numbers rather than colouring outside the lines on their own terms. But I can't quantify it for you. All I know is, more often than not, readers just know whether the writer is having a good time.

So, why not have a good time?

After all, as far as I know, nobody has a gun to your head demanding that you write a novel this year. Or a play. Or a poem. And if you are looking for ways to get published, the odds are at this stage you are not making a significant amount of money from the writing process. Which means you come to the blank page voluntarily. Giving yourself an incentive to keep returning to the blank page voluntarily is often the difference between abandoning a writing project halfway through and finishing it. And I'm proposing that one of the best incentives for all of us is happiness; a feeling deep down that we are spending our time how we want to spend it.

Thus, if you find joy between the pages – even if it's the joy of terrifying yourself with a spooky story, the joy of relief as you tell a real-life tale that you've been aching to share or the joy of living vicariously through characters who are much braver than you – the odds are the reader will find joy in your work as well. Given that editors and agents are readers too, this can only work to your advantage in achieving your goal of becoming a published writer.

CHAPTER 2: THE FULL-TIME WRITER

"The hardest thing about being a writer is convincing your wife that lying on the sofa is work." **– John Hughes.**

One of the most damaging concepts I have ever come across as a creative writing tutor is the idea of the 'full-time writer.' In almost every class, in almost every genre, from poetry to fantasy fiction, this idea will present itself. Usually, right after I ask the class what they would like to get out of the workshop, someone will raise their hand and say: 'I'd like to know how to become a full-time writer.' Or 'I'd like to know how you manage to complete projects when you are not a full-time writer.' These statements, and statements like them, never cease to astound me no matter how many times I hear them.

It astounds me because it is proof that on some level there are many people out there who still think of the role of a writer in what might readily be described as 19th Century terms. That is to say, there are people who still think of writers as reclusive hermits who do nothing but sit at a desk and write from dawn until dusk. And we presumably think that our financial options are the same as they were in the 19th Century too: that we either have to starve for our craft or need to be one of those lucky, financially independent individuals who has received monies from a generous benefactor and thus can spend each day however we please.

Mercifully, what it means to be a writer has moved on a bit since the 19th Century.

But before we explore that, I'm going to suggest a shift in perspective that might help ease some of the imposter syndrome that plagues writers who do not spend ten hours a day chained to their computer, writing books.

What if I told you that you could become a full-time writer right now, regardless of how much time you spent at the keyboard in the last week? Would you be interested in that? Surely any lover of the craft would be. I certainly would have been if somebody had asked me that question fifteen years ago.

Before I explain how, let me ask you a question: if you did spend all of yesterday writing, when you went to bed for some much-needed shut-eye, did you stop being a writer for those next eight hours? If you are a dad, did you stop being a dad, or a daughter, or a teacher for those eight hours also?

Can we all agree that the fair answer to that question is no? You may not be actively parenting or teaching or writing in your sleep, but that doesn't mean you cease to identify with that label – which is, in the most reductive sense, what these things are. They are identifiers so that people we socialise with and work with can figure out which box we fit into. They are also identifiers we latch onto to shape our perception of who we are.

If you are a father full-time, whether you are at this very moment giving your kid mediocre advice on their homework that you're doing your best to pass off as top-level tutoring, why aren't you a full-time writer whether or not you're sitting at the keyboard?

I have an answer for you. You may have your own answer, but here's mine: unless you are one of the few big names that people inevitably drop when discussing writer success stories, such as Stephen King, John Grisham or Nora Roberts, being a writer is an uncertain business. For those of us who do not have a long-term, proven track record, and a back catalogue of books to prove it, writing falls into that beautiful spectrum of the unknown. The unknown is an exciting place, but it's not one in which you can make bankable predictions. Consequently, the part of our brain that is wired for survival hates the unquantifiable and in order to protect you it will do everything in its power to keep you well away from the ghastly, the unthinkable unknown.

In my imagining this part of the brain is voiced by a withered old hobgoblin. He has gleaming yellow eyes and a raspy voice. The goblin's tactics include convincing you that you are not a full-time writer because you only have three hours a week to give to your craft, so you might as well not even try being successful at it. The goblin-voiced, survival part of your brain would love to keep you safely locked up in that cocoon of disbelief, but unfortunately this cocoon is not as comfortable as our survival instincts would have us think. Although it saves us from rejection and financial uncertainty, it also suffocates the creative soul. For those of us born with a desire to create beautiful and meaningful things, that is one of the worst feelings in the world.

Why do I think this is the reason we criticize ourselves for not being full-time writers? I happen to have a lot of experience facing down this primitive part of my brain. Growing up, I was lucky to be best friends with a girl whose mother ran self-development classes with an organization called *More to Life*. In my early 20s I completed several courses with the *More to Life* programme, including self-esteem courses, the *More to Life* weekend and a residential course that took place on the outskirts of Atlanta, Georgia called *Way of the Warrior*. I'm well aware of how hokey this might sound to some readers. But that's all right. I'm OK with you thinking it's a little hokey because it helped me. And sometimes a little bit of hokey doesn't hurt.

On these courses, we took part in activities that by some people's standards would be considered mad. We agreed to give up all stimulants for the duration of the course: coffee, Coca Cola, chocolate, you name it. We shouted at invisible opponents at the top of our lungs. On the residential course we agreed to have our rooms subjected to military style-inspections and danced around in nothing but our swimwear until late into the night.

See, I told you: mad.

Or maybe I've just lived a very sheltered life and you're sitting there thinking 'that's not mad, Helen. That's just a regular Saturday night for me.' If you live your life on the edge this way, I salute you.

Either way, I can tell you that a lot of these things were way out of my comfort zone, and that was the point. Every activity we took part in was designed to push our buttons so the survival part of our brain would kick in and stop us from trying new stuff. After all, you can only chop the head off the subterranean monster if it sticks its head out of the dirt.

I spent several years acknowledging and coming to terms with the fact that this part of my mind really existed. I just wasn't conscious of its influence before. If you've ever told yourself that you're 'always going to fail' or you'll 'never be a real writer' or anything else that has kept you from taking a leap that might ultimately make you feel more alive, you'll be well-acquainted with the cynical narrator, that sly goblin voice that seems to be well-meaning but ultimately keeps you from achieving the goals that will make you happiest in this world.

But back to my original promise - to transform you into a full-time writer in a matter of seconds.

Ready to shape-shift?

As you may have gathered from my facetious question regarding whether you stop being a father or an accountant just because you dare to catch up on some much needed kip, I am not of the opinion that you are only a writer during the minutes you sit at a desk writing. Just as there may be times when you're not around your kids but are still processing and planning elements of your parenthood, there may be times when you are not sitting at your desk writing when you are processing and planning elements of your work. Being a writer requires the gathering of experiences. It requires taking some time to observe and immerse yourself in the world around you. It sometimes demands that you read several novels or non-fiction volumes just to be able to write with some degree of awareness the genre you are writing in.

In fairness, most writers I know can make peace with the idea that reading is part of the writing process and counts as time spent 'being a writer.' What they often discount as though it were of no use to their greater purpose is the day job. Most people think of the day job as an annoyance that steals their time away from writing. I felt this way for many years. Between the ages of twenty-one and thirty-five I was convinced that every minute spent doing something other than writing was a minute I spent getting further away from my dreams.

It was only when I had my first romance novel published that I understood how useful the various life experiences I'd had were to my craft. The novel takes place at a 1950s themed diner in New York and the central character was an English teacher turned waitress. I had about fifteen years of waitress experience to my name and had taught English in schools for about seven years. The money I made from my day job had enabled me to travel to New

York on more than one occasion – a city I instantly fell in love with and which still holds a very special place in my heart. Let's also not forget the fact that writing with accuracy and precision was a built-in part of many of the day jobs I took. Writing menus, emails and reports – all of it was covert writing practise, I just didn't choose to view it that way at the time.

When the reviews of my first novel came in, most of them noted how vivid the descriptions of New York were. Many thought that I had lived in New York when, in fact, I'd just been on a few trips there. I highly doubt I would have been able to write about a city I wasn't native to with such confidence if I'd never visited it. And I never would have been able to visit it without the funds from my day job. Similarly, I never would have been able to write convincingly about what it's like to do an eight hour waitressing shift in heels had I not done it myself for years. The publishing of my first novel was a landmark moment in so many respects. Possibly the most valuable thing I took away from that experience, however, was the realisation that as a writer every experience, no matter what it is, can be put to use in our work. Part of the challenge when juggling our lives alongside the writing is to figure out how we can use the experiences we have as the starting point for some great material.

The benefits of taking this approach to writing go beyond a greater appreciation of the life you are already leading – which is of course important in its own right. Embracing this perspective can actually improve and enrich the work you produce. When discussing this idea with my students I often quote a line from *The Bell Jar* by Sylvia Plath, a barely-fictionalised account of a summer she spent in New York City. In the book, the narrator is trying to write a novel, and she comments dryly: *"How could I write about life when I'd never had a love affair or a baby or seen anybody die?"*

When I started out as a writer I very much related to this point of view. For a girl who had been writing stories since she was old enough to hold a pen, the next logical step on deciding to become a writer would surely be to stay at home and live with my parents. That way I could sit at my laptop and write several books without having to concern myself with trivial matters like rent or buying food or paying the electric bill. But that's not what I did.

For one thing, I was far too set on being financially independent to even think about living with my parents. For another, if I was going to write for something other than my own amusement, well, frankly I had no idea what I should write about. I hadn't been out in the world long enough to know where my obsessions and fascinations lay. I hadn't yet had some of the most important formative experiences that would shape my later stories.

In short, regardless of the genre you are writing in, experience in the world is a real asset to a writer's difficult to clock up that life experience if you have barricaded yourself into a room to write for ten hours a day.

Besides giving you a deeper appreciation of the life you are already leading and enriching the stories you will go on to write, treating each experience as a valuable source of material also means that once you do get time to sit down and write it is highly unlikely that you'll suffer from blocks. If you've kept notes or jotted down observations, dictated important strands of dialogue into your phone or even made a mental note to use a particular image or experience as a starting point for a piece of writing, then the blank page will not hold much terror for you.

Thus, I encourage you to think of writing as more than the act of putting words on the page – though undoubtedly a book or poem or memoir or script cannot be finished unless you do just that at some point. Instead, think of writing as an ongoing quest for information and material for use in those precious moments when you do have a notebook or laptop in front of you. Not every situation is going to be a Pulitzer Prize winning scenario without some manipulation or dramatization. But turning our experience into something compelling and unforgettable is an excellent starting challenge for any writer.

So next time you spend the afternoon you'd set aside for writing taking your dog to the vet, try not to resent the poor pooch. You never know, an adventure into the world of veterinary science might be just the inspiration you need to spark your next creative project.

CHAPTER 3: PURPOSE

"The purpose of life is a life of purpose." – **Robert Byrne.**

Do you have a clear sense of purpose in your writing? Do you know why you want to do this rather than paint or run a marathon or become an award-winning chef? Maybe you do all those other things as a side-line. Certainly one does not negate the other. But when it comes to sitting down at a computer or with a pen in hand and putting words on the page, do you know why you do it?

While writing the hundreds of chapters, articles and poems I've produced over the years, I came to realise that knowing why I was writing spurred me towards completion like nothing else.

I first learned this lesson from novelist and poet Kate North, who taught on the MA course I completed at the University of York St John in 2006. She insisted that when you were writing a poem, you should ask yourself 'so what?' after each line. These weren't necessarily the words a group of self-indulgent writers in their early twenties wanted to hear, but it was what we all needed to hear. Because asking 'so what?' after each line of poetry I wrote got me into the habit of questioning my 'why?'.

Purpose will differ for each writer and will probably develop as we mature. Purpose can also differ for each piece of work. The most common gut response you'll get from writers when you ask them why they do it is that they have to write. They can't tell you exactly why they feel this way, they just know that writing, for them, is a lot like breathing and going too long without doing it has dire consequences for their wellbeing.

Although I relate to this whole-heartedly, I also think it's useful to push ourselves beyond this stock answer in order to enrich our work and better understand our desire to realise it.

I encourage you to think about this topic, nay write about this topic, on several levels, starting with the general. Why are you drawn to writing? Does it provide a meaningful escape from other elements of 21st century living? Is the page the only place you can say what you think without being interrupted? Is it your best chance of being heard because generally people don't care too much for what you have to say? Is it your most comfortable means of connection with other human beings? Is it a creative pursuit replacing a career that you've now retired from, if so, why writing and not basket weaving? The list goes on. Your general writing purpose could be any of these things or more than one of them, or none of them. We are all individuals and we each have our own unique path into this kind of work.

As an exercise, try setting a timer for ten minutes and writing non-stop. Start with the sentence 'I write because...' and keep the pen moving. This piece of writing is for you. Nobody else is going to see it or, more importantly, judge it. So you can write uncensored. When you do this, I'm going to ask you not to try and be profound or witty or clever – though I'm very sure you are all those things. I'm going to ask you <u>not</u> to focus on finding the perfect word or creating ornate sentences. I'm asking you just to tell the truth as you feel it now, in this moment.

Once you've written about this on a more general basis, you can complete the same task for every specific piece of writing before you start writing it, or if you get stuck or demotivated along the way. Developing your understanding of purpose in relation to a specific project can further help to shape the work you produce. For example, in the summer of 2019, I produced a short collection of poems inspired by Native American imagery. I dedicated the pamphlet to my late Aunt Shirley who, in 1988, travelled from Eagle Rock, California, to marry my uncle Ray. She lived out the rest of her years in Middlesbrough which, for non-UK readers, is in the north east of England. Moving there from Los Angeles would have been quite the culture shift. Shirley had Apache ancestry and in writing the pamphlet of poems I hoped to honour and preserve that part of our extended family history. That was my why. And thinking about Shirley's transatlantic journey helped to shape the poems. Knowing that, when I'd finished the project, there would be something concrete to commemorate her life also encouraged me to see the work through to completion.

Your purpose doesn't have to be as 'serious' as this. I also write very light-hearted murder mystery novels where my purpose is to provide the reader with some much-needed escapism. So if you're struggling with a project and finding it hard to get motivated or to finish the last few chapters, I recommend sitting down with your writing equipment and spilling ink for ten minutes about why you want to create this piece and why you feel it's worth putting it out there in the world. What kind of pleasure, solace, insight, guidance or information will your reader find in the work? Why do you want to be the one to provide it?

In the 2019 movie *A Star is Born* – a film in which Bradley Cooper plays a rock star that I watched for purely academic reasons, honest – there is an altercation between two brothers. Bobby, played by Sam Elliot, is resentful towards Jack, played by Bradley Cooper, because of his musical success. The argument goes back and forth for a short while before Jack spits at his brother: 'You had nothing to fucking say.' This is Jack, who is struggling with alcoholism, in one of his coldest moments. Even though his delivery could do with some refining, he had a point. He's suggesting that his brother could write mediocre, forgettable songs but doesn't have anything to say that listeners can connect with. Again, what you have to say need not be deep and meaningful. A desire to celebrate frivolity or the lighter elements in life is in itself a purpose. Creative works with no clear purpose however can often feel forgettable because there is no underlying idea, no heart for the reader to connect with.

For those of you concerned about it, just because you have a plain purpose doesn't mean you have to bash your reader over the head with it. There are subtle ways of working your purpose through a story, poem, script or song through theme, setting, character and plot. So don't let the fear of seeming like a sanctimonious old fool put you off – that's your editor's problem. Well, and then your problem once they hand you the notes but the point is, that's fixable. Much more fixable than trying to artificially inject heart into a piece of writing that has none.

So before you write your magnum opus, or if you get stuck part way, ask yourself: do you have something to say? And, just as importantly, do you have the courage to say it? More about finding that courage in the next chapter...

CHAPTER 4: COURAGE

"It's [courage] from the Latin word cor, meaning heart — and the original definition was to tell the story of who you are with your whole heart." – **Brené Brown.**

I loved this definition of courage, as explained by Brené Brown from the first moment I heard it. It was handy for gently breaking it to students who had decided to write autobiographical stories that they had, in fact, selected the most difficult genre to write in. A piece of information that did not make me particularly popular but was, I felt, important to flag up in my creative non-fiction classes.

Non-fiction arguably calls us to be courageous more than any other genre because, despite current criticisms about the inaccuracies in reportage from the world's press, writing non-fiction means that you are bound by fact and truth. There is no making up characters or scenarios, at least not without declaring it in your introduction and offering a jolly good reason for the deceit. There is no portraying yourself as less sulky or more athletic. Or making out that the first person you slept with was some firmly sculpted Adonis rather than the guy with hairy hands that worked behind the counter at the local chippie. Non-fiction writers have a contract with the reader to tell them to truth or at the very least be very up front about anything they've fudged in the name of artistic flourish. Telling the whole truth about who we are and the choices we've made takes true courage.

But it's not just non-fiction writers who need to lean into courage in order to produce work. One of the scariest aspects of writing is that the page can often feel like a stage where you, the writer, stand front and centre. Your audience is, in your mind, a hoard of frothing critics who will not only pick you up on how unoriginal your metaphors are but will see straight through your thinly-veiled story about a man who grew up on the outskirts of Slough in Thatcher's Britain and started his own line of solar-powered dishwashers. 'You grew up on the outskirts of Slough in Thatcher's Britain,' they'll jeer, 'this story is really about you, isn't it?'

If there's one thing I've learnt from my time as a published writer, it's that no matter how fictional your story is, readers, bloggers and interviewers will always want to get to the bottom of one question: how much is this book about you? What's real? What's true? This has happened when I've written stories and poems about English maidens crossing the Atlantic and falling in love with Native American men, when I've written about librarians who solve murder mysteries as a side-gig and when I've written from the perspective of mythological characters.

For the record, I am not a mythological being. Though I had an American aunt with Apache heritage, I've never met a man with Native American heritage in person. And as far as I recall, I've never cracked a murder case with the help of a lovable side-kick. Though of course, I wish I could lay claim to all of these assertions. I have to admit, however, that it would be disingenuous of me to say that the books were not about me. Or that there wasn't any of me in them. But it's not the logistics. I don't think anyone needs to read a book about a woman who wakes up, eats her cereal, watches some cute puppy videos on Instagram and then sits down to work at a laptop for seven hours save a walk around midday. And sure, not every day of my life looks like that, and it is a reductive view of me as a person, but day-to-day the plot is pretty thin.

What is rich, however, is the interior life. The thoughts, the feelings, the memories, the dreams, the fantasies, the bonds, and the relationships. And so, when I answer questions about how close my books are to my real life, I explain this distinction. The physical aspects of the book may be far-fetched and implausible (highly likely if I'm writing the book as escapism is my thing) but there is an emotional truth to them. For who hasn't, in their lifetime, brushed up against fear, despair, elation and delight? Our emotions are part of what makes us human. And, as such, even if the scenario I present to the reader is ridiculous, in the spirit of entertainment, they will still connect with it if the emotional truth is present. That part of my writing is straight from my heart.

In this respect, writers can wear fiction like a mask and masks can help us draw on our courage. There's a reason why most superheroes wear them. And Westley in *The Princess Bride* assures us that they are very comfortable. You can create fictional scenarios that do not in any way reflect your personal experience, that are born of uncensored imagination but allow you to write about the most exhilarating and frightening moments you've ever experienced. If you can write with emotional honesty, you will add a real depth to your work. You will have honoured the truth inside you that you wanted to explore. But you will also provide yourself with a convenient veil to slip behind when discussing your work. You can say things like: 'At this point the character feels like there is no way out. That's a feeling I relate to and I'm sure lots of others do too,' or 'The speaker in this poem is trying to move out of a lonely space into one of connection.' That's very different to saying. 'This actually happened to me and I faithfully transcribed the experience into my work.' A sentence that will surely beg lots of intimate questions we may not be comfortable with.

I often tell my students that fiction is the manipulation of fact to reveal truth. And I think we can draw courage from that idea. It offers us a degree of control over what we share with readers. It reminds me that I don't have to share every little detail about who I am and what I stand for in each piece of work I produce. I can control what I share, how much I share, and when I share it. But, I would caution you about only instilling your characters with your best attributes. About only sharing the optimum version of yourself with the reader. This links with something else I always tell my students: if you want to make your job really hard, write about super-nice people who always do the right thing, never over-react and have all the answers.

Regardless of how highly we esteem ourselves, most of us would have to admit that this isn't a very accurate description of the average person and thus fiction needs to reflect this. We need characters who make mistakes, say the wrong thing and jump off the deep end when something rattles them. Just like the rest of us most likely have done at some point during our life. This will mean drawing on personal experience where you didn't get it right. When you either didn't know any better or could have done better. Most of us would prefer to hide these parts of ourselves away so we could escape judgement over them but I promise you that won't endear readers to either you or your characters. As human beings, if there's one thing we're not that keen on, it's being presented with the perfect vision of a person who can't put a foot wrong. It doesn't make us feel particularly good about ourselves and, though I haven't looked it up in any writing self-help books, I suspect generating a feeling of inadequacy in your reader probably isn't the best way to encourage them to relate.

I could have written this book without conveying to you any of my embarrassing writerly moments or by skipping over the low parts of my writing career. But I don't think that would help you connect with me or what I'm trying to say. I also think some part of you would either resent me for seemingly having had it so easy or suspect me of not telling my whole truth, as Brené Brown's explanation of the word courage demands. And you would be right. I would be short-changing you, fooling you even. My writing career has not been perfect. I am not perfect. I've made many mistakes and although they are quite mortifying to admit at times, I am taking a leap and trusting that you value my authenticity over all else.

This is an important leap to make with your readership. There is something intimate about the act of reading. Although lots of other people might have read the same book as you, when you read it for yourself it's just you and the writer. Just the two of you in a cosy exchange of ideas. That reader has the choice of many thousands of books, but they chose to read yours. When a reader shows that trust in you, it's only fair to show a certain level of trust in return and write with a degree of honesty. Assuming they finish your book, the reader is going to spend a good few hours with you and nobody wants to spend time with a phoney.

So wear the mask of fiction, or take the heart-thundering leap of writing non-fiction and laying yourself completely bare. But whichever route you choose, remember that authenticity is a rare quality and its scarcity makes it valuable. If you can offer the reader a glimpse of your authentic self, you will build a long-lasting trust with them that will make exploring even your darkest thoughts and emotions on the page seem less scary. Displaying this level of courage and honesty for the enjoyment and solace of others is surely the best method of touching another human being without ever meeting them.

CHAPTER 5: TOUGH LOVE

"Discomfort is the price of admission to a meaningful life." – **Susan David.**

At the tender age of six I spent a summer's day lolling in the back garden behind the bungalow my parents owned in rural Cumbria. I don't know why that sunny day in 1987 seemed like such a fine time to make some big life choices. I was a peculiarly introspective child, which might have had a little something to do with it. At any rate, that's how I passed the time until supper was ready. I made these big life choices the way I imagine most six-year-olds make big life choices, which is to say I lied out on a bed of freshly-cut grass, watching the clouds roll on while thinking about what I could do with my time here that would make me happy.

Time works differently when you're six. My recollection is that I spent hours out there pondering. My memory is that Aristotle had nothing on me. In truth, probably less than two hours had passed before I returned from my period of deep thinking and announced to my northern, working-class parents that I had decided to become a writer. My parents, fearing their first-born was likely to starve to death in such an uncertain business, told me that writing was a nice hobby. It would be a pleasant way to pass evenings and weekends after I had worked my contracted forty-hours at a proper day job. At the time I accepted this response because I assumed, in that self-absorbed, arrogant manner children do, that I knew better than my parents. My plan was to progress from celebrated macaroni artist to the Nobel Prize winner for literature in record time. Hey, at least you can't fault my levels of ambition. I had faith that I could make this dream happen without the need for a soul-sucking day job.

To some of you, age six is going to seem a little early to have your life plan mapped out, but it's not uncommon. If Mozart could learn to play both the piano and the violin by the age of four, then it's surely easy to believe that a non-child-prodigy such as myself could figure out that I enjoyed writing stories by the age of six. Even if at that point the only substantial piece I'd finished was a short fantasy work of three pages that was heavily derivative of *The Wizard of Oz*. Most people who were creative from an early age will tell you some form of this story: of confessing their deepest hope to create worlds and characters on the page and in response hearing someone close to them say that it's not going to happen.

Rarely is early suppression enough to stop a truly determined creative soul however, and in most cases it only makes us more insistent that we are going to be creative. Consequences and invitations to Christmas dinner be damned. Perhaps then, it's not too surprising that by the time I hit my teenage years my creative tenancies had become a touchy subject in my household. My parents did all they could to steer me towards a sensible and certain mode of existence where I would not need to worry about the inconsistencies of book sales or publishing market trends. My teachers held little hope of a grand literary career for me either. Some of them thought I would do well to get a job at the local bank or on the till at the pharmacy in the market square. Not that there's anything wrong with those jobs, but I knew even then that the kind of work I wanted to do was creative. From my point of view, the path marked out by teachers and parents was akin to a slow emotional death. As I only had limited say in what I did with my life at that point, I had little choice but to go along with their suggestions hoping I would be able to live a more authentic life later when I had more control over my day-to-day dealings.

Those of you who didn't start on the creative path until later might wonder why a parent or teacher would decide to drive a child off their desired creative path. Though it felt adversarial at the time (thanks a bunch teenage hormones!) they did not act out of cruelty. As a writer, or indeed an artist of any kind, you will at some point find somebody who will tell you that you are striving for the impossible. That you cannot do what you want to do. They will tell you that you will fail. That you will be penniless and miserable and that your work will count for nothing. In the case of my parents, they were scared of their child becoming what they frequently described as 'a drifter'. They weren't just talking about the possibility of being homeless or poor, they were referring also to a person who drifts through life without any real purpose or making any real contribution.

If you think about it from their point of view, particularly in the age I grew up in – before the dawn of the internet and the self-publishing revolution – their fears were entirely understandable. They weren't trying to deter me because they didn't want me to be happy. Rather, they were trying to achieve my happiness through means they had tested themselves. It wasn't cruelty; it was love. Tough love, but love nonetheless.

I can't blame my teachers for being dubious about my literary aspirations, either. Sure, I got good grades in English and always wrote a poem for school performance evenings, but on the whole my academic achievements could be slotted into the good category rather than outstanding. I always got passing grades and my attendance record was strong – but these are hardly the hallmarks of literary greatness. My teachers were no doubt concerned that encouraging me to walk a creative path where my mediocrity might only be emphasised would be hurtful and destructive to me and my future.

There was one thing my parents and teachers didn't factor in, however: how badly I wanted to be a writer. My determination to realise my dreams smashed all of their well-meaning doubts to pieces. They couldn't have anticipated this, and, to be honest, neither could I. I spent the vast majority of my teen years and my twenties thinking they were right in their assessments. I wrote and wrote but I did it without ever really believing I was going to make it as a published writer. Sheer persistence and craft practise however, was enough for me to surpass the expectations of those who knew me when I was young. But there were no guarantees that it would happen and still, even now, no guarantees it will last. I've made my peace with that uncertainty but having danced for fifteen years or so without knowing where the next step will take me, I can see why my parents and teachers were ushering me towards working the till at the local pharmacy.

Thus when the people you love, the people who in your fantasies are the most supportive of your dream, tell you this isn't something you should pursue take heart in the fact that what sounds like a distinct lack of faith in you and your creative abilities is actually an expression of love. And a reflection of their worst fears for someone they love so dearly. They don't want you to meet with the many things you will undoubtedly face as a writer: rejection, criticism, uncertainty. They want to keep you safe, even if that safety means you miss out on a glorious adventure. Do them and yourselves a favour and don't hate them for it. Maybe just find other people to talk with about your passion and look forward to the expression on their faces when your book is finally out and they have to admit that you could do it after all.

Vengeful? Me? Never.

Now, of course, not everyone who tells you you'll fail is doing so out of love. Some people are acting out of jealousy; out of the need to feel more powerful than you or because they are all round more sensible folk less prone to flighty behaviour. The kind of person who frowns on other people taking unpredictable journeys they cannot relate to. The views of such individuals are often more difficult to manage as deep down you know their comments aren't coming from a 'good place'. That for whatever reason, they're not 'on your side.' The key point to note here is that their insistence that you will fail says a lot more about them than it does about you. They are being ruled by their own agendas and by their own fears. Take inspiration from the fact that you are not following the same path they've chosen. That you are taking fear along for the ride, because that's part of an adventure, but you are not being ruled by it. And with such individuals always, always remember: they cannot predict your future and they have no idea what you are capable of. Neither will you unless you ignore their negativity and keep trying.

Although opposition to your craft can prove trying overall, you can help yourself by not viewing it as a negative thing. Sometimes, I wonder what would have happened if my parents had been on board with my writing from the day I first announced my interest in it. In my imaginings, I would have been mollycoddled. I would have stayed at home to write and live with my parents until my books had taken off. And yes, I would have had time to practise my craft at a much younger age but I do wonder if the books would really have been 'about anything'. If I had done that I wouldn't actually have anything to write about except how amazing our Mam's cheese scones are and though they are cheesy morsels of inspiration unto themselves, I probably couldn't get more than a poetry pamphlet out of that.

If I'd lived at home and locked myself in a room to write, I wouldn't have known what it was like to leave everything behind for a big city like London. I wouldn't have had the money to travel to unknown places and soak up new cultures. If I'd never left home and got jobs I didn't like and had experiences in the world and met people who were vastly different to the people I grew up with, I would likely be writing stories about people like me and that material would have dried up pretty fast. Ultimately, whether or not I like it, the tough love I received around my desire to be creative propelled me out into the world and made me into the writer I have become.

Having somebody turn around and say directly that you're going to fail, or that you're not a real writer unless you're published or any of the many hurtful things that can fall out of some people's mouth, seemingly without them batting an eyelid, isn't really what any of us want to hear. But how you receive such words can make a vast difference to your creative life. When it does happen, rather than becoming bitter or angry, you could choose to interpret it as life pushing back, levelling up to you and asking: are you serious about this writing thing? How serious? What will you do to make it happen? What will you sacrifice? Can you cope with a little of resistance?

In my case, the answer was always the same. No matter what the obstacle, my answer remained yes.

Viewing the people who try to deter you from following your creative passions as deliverers of necessary resistance frees you to take their comments much more lightly. It invites you to recommit to creation, regardless of the challenges, and often provides you with some interesting character material.

In the long-term, experiences like these also teach you that you know yourself better than anyone else and ultimately the only voice you have to listen to is the one deep inside. Your intuition guiding you towards the life you want most, no matter what anyone else has to say about it.

CHAPTER 6: ORIGINALITY

"You're born an original, don't die a copy." **John L. Mason.**

Does the pressure of creating original material ever impede your writing? Given how many books, TV shows and films have been made it can sometimes feel like there is little fresh territory to explore. As such, when we sit down to work, we can find ourselves plagued with questions that stand firmly in the way of our productivity. Questions like: how can I make sure my story matters? Or, how can I make sure my story resonates? Perhaps the first step when we feel this kind of pressure is to recognise that just because there are other similar stories out there, doesn't mean that our story is devoid of originality.

Not convinced? Let's take an example from my own experience as a novelist.

My first fiction publisher Harper Collins scheduled my debut novel, a romance set in a 1950s-themed diner, for release in July 2016. That same summer established author Samantha Tonge released her novella: *How to Get Hitched in 10 Days*. It was also a romance set at a 1950s-themed diner.

On the surface, these books sound very similar but if you read both you would understand them to be very different pieces of work before you had even reached the bottom of the first page. Samantha's story is set in England, mine is set in America. Samantha's has a light, almost whimsical tone, mine has a suspense edge. Hers is contemporary, mine was set in 1990. Between us, Samantha and I turned what some might have deemed an 'unfortunate clash' into a marketing opportunity by merrily cross-promoting our books to each other's readership. Both we and the readers were happy. Everybody won.

The big lesson I took away from this experience, besides how cool and collaborative the author community can be, is that even if someone writes a work that looks similar to yours, at a deeper level the stories will not resemble each other. This is because the title of this chapter is a bit of a cheat. I don't need to teach you how to be original. You already are.

You are unique. Nobody in the world is a carbon copy of your good self, which means nobody can write the same story as you in the way that you will write it. I have always found that quite an inspiring thought. Especially as a person who writes genre fiction, the section of the bookshop that is arguably most often accused of lacking originality. When I write my murder mystery novels, you will see some familiar components, but there is no doubt that those books have my individual imprint on them. Someone else could try to copy that but would never fully replicate my own unique style. In short, nobody else will arrange words on a page quite the way you do. You've also got your own inspirations, personal experiences, points of reference and messages you want to convey to the reader that differentiate you from other writers. If you stay true to these, what you create will always be original.

If you are concerned that you might be inadvertently copying another person's style to lesser effect, rather than leaning into your own unique voice, then you could take a different tack. Seek to become actively conscious of how you blend the accepted components of a story or poem. We are all working with roughly the same elements after all. Just as musicians are working with a fixed set of musical notes, painters with a fixed set of colours and chefs with a fixed set of ingredients. What makes a creation unique is *the way* in which those ingredients are blended. How much cayenne pepper? How little salt? What about finding a tasty way to mix peanut butter and apple sauce? (I promise I am a much better cook than this analogy suggests).

If you want to be more active about originality, then set out a list of ingredients you're working with in your chosen genre and pay attention to how you are twisting them in ways readers have been less exposed to. Get playful enough and you might even invent a new subgenre.

The next paragraph is a shameless name drop, but it's totally relevant, honest.

One time I gate-crashed an after party at a science-fiction convention (because I was THAT cool in my twenties). I got talking to Simon Pegg, as you do, who was excitedly showing me a bunch of photographs on his phone from a new movie he was shooting. That movie became *Sean of the Dead* but he didn't use that title when he talked to me about it. When I asked what the film was about, he said it was a 'Zom-Rom-Com.' That genre didn't exist at the time.

It does now.

If all of the above still doesn't settle your nerves about being original, perhaps you can take solace in the following point. While working on any given piece of writing, if you're doing your research right, you will probably find out that someone has already published something similar to what you're working on. Reading that work is useful in ascertaining how that author covered that topic. If you read several milestone books in the genre you are writing, you will quickly get a sense of the common themes and tropes. This will in turn give you some sense of what you could do differently. Sure, it can be intimidating reading the polished work of other people who have made a name for themselves in an area you are trying to break into. But what you are reading is precisely that: a polished piece of writing that will have gone through many drafts and rewrites, just as your work will.

Thus, you shouldn't feel *so* intimidated by the mere existence of other works in the genre that you decide against writing the stories you want to write. Just because something similar exists already doesn't mean that readers won't enjoy your work – in fact in all likelihood the opposite is true. Other authors have essentially done you a big favour and awakened a readership to the kind of story you are now writing. So, if anything, particularly in a world where publishers are only interested in taking very calculated risks, similarities between your work and that of other writers are to be welcomed rather than feared.

CHAPTER 7: BLOCKS

"If you find a path with no obstacles, it probably doesn't lead anywhere." – **Frank A. Clark.**

Perhaps one of the biggest mistakes writers make when trying to tackle writer's block is to view it as one overarching, all-consuming problem. Viewed this way, a block can quickly become our own personal yellow-fanged poltergeist hiding under the shift key on our keyboard. Lurking in its nest of broken dreams and discarded polystyrene cups until it hears us say those immortal words: 'I think I'll get some writing done.'

This approach not only makes the block seem undefeatable but also prevents us from getting to the root cause of the block. In truth, writer's block is an umbrella term for several different factors that might prevent a writer from moving forward with a project. I cannot profess to know them all because writers are individuals and are thus likely to encounter blocks unique to them. But I can apprise you of the most common forms a block can take and offer you strategies to push past them.

The most common, and perhaps most simple kind of block to fix, is the feeling of not having any ideas. That familiar experience of sitting in front of an impatient cursor, every blink a challenge to your creative genius. If you experience this kind of block, the solution is fairly straightforward. Remember what I said about writing being the kind of career that doesn't lend itself to sitting around waiting for your ship to come in? This is the sort of situation I was thinking of. If no ideas are coming to you, you need to go out and generate them. Swim out to your ship and meet it. This might involve setting a timer and handwriting non-stop about things that have fascinated you, scared you, inspired you or touched you in the past. You can fill those pages with absolutely anything you want. Anything that captivates you. So write about the most exciting place you ever visited or a dream place you want to visit. Write about why that place entices you, how you imagine it, and once you have exhausted all your own ideas, start researching that place. Read books, watch TV shows and movies that are set there. Watch documentaries about its history. Congratulations. You now not only have a setting for your story but you have likely unearthed several story possibilities simply by doing your research.

When we suffer blocks like this, we put pressure on ourselves to be some kind of magic ideas machine. It is not your responsibility to create out of thin air. Instead, absorb, internalise and synthesise. If you find yourself blocked in this way, it's time to spark your curiosity and fall in love with a place, a time, a person, or an ideal and chase the stories that surround it.

And while we're on the subject of pressure, I can tell you with some confidence that sitting down to write and telling yourself you're going to write the most amazing work of literature the world has ever seen is a sure-fire way of getting yourself blocked before the end of chapter one. Seriously, writing is hard enough without unnecessarily raising the stakes like that. If this is your first novel or your third short story or your fifth poem then isn't it unreasonable to expect literary perfection at this stage? It doesn't really matter how far through your writing career you are. On the whole, like anyone else repeatedly coming back to a craft or task, you will have good days and bad days and as a consequence your expectations need to be fair.

How about instead of sitting down to write the greatest story ever told, you sit down to write a story that amuses you, or moves you? How about sitting down to tell a story that you think will move or amuse others? Maybe you even have a specific person in mind when you're writing. If so, as you write, add in jokes or plot twists you know would appeal to you and them.

I'll level with you. I once sat down to write the greatest work of literature the world had ever seen. I got to chapter eighteen, had a falling out with my protagonist – as only a writer could – and abandoned the project. That story had real potential, but I was taking it far too seriously. And the protagonist was taking herself far too seriously to the point that she wouldn't really do anything that was worth a reader's precious time. Maybe someday I'll revisit that idea but because I associate it with drab solemnity, I'm not itching to go back to it in the way I think I should be if I ever want to serve it up to my readership.

A few years later, I sat down to write a bad romance book. That's how I talked about it. Yes, that's right, I set the standard so low for myself I was fairly sure even I couldn't fail on this one. And do you know how it felt to be writing something 'bad'? Really, really good.

I didn't have to impress anyone. I didn't have to write ornate prose (though I have read a lot of Daphne du Maurier and had a crack at that anyway). I didn't have to do anything witty or profound. I could just write a story from the point of view of a character whose voice I couldn't get out of my head. I didn't even know it was going to be 'a novel' when I started writing it. I thought it might be a short story, maybe a novella – I even set the word count bar low.

Seventy-five thousand words later, I had the first draft of a novel. And you know what? It wasn't *that* bad. I began polishing the story and six months later signed a contract with Harper Collins. Until I'd finished the first draft, I didn't take the job seriously. I revelled in it. And that's when it hit me: if I stopped taking my writing *quite* so seriously, writing could feel like this all the time. And why wouldn't I want that? Why wouldn't any creative person?

So if you find yourself blocked and can't quite put your finger on why, stop for a moment and ask yourself: how much pressure is there here? How seriously am I taking it? Is there a way of setting the initial bar a bit lower so I'm not so intimidated that I can't even put words – even bad words – down on the page?

The third and final form of block I'm going to explore is the one that often strikes when a project is par-cooked. I'm talking about that moment where everything seems to be going well with the project and then suddenly you hit a wall that you can't seem to move past. For whatever reason, you can't find a segue into the next line, paragraph or chapter. How you move past such a wall will vastly depend on what kind of work you're doing. Non-fiction writers often hit a wall when more research is required. If you aren't clear on a particular matter or incident, then how are you supposed to convey it to a reader in a precise manner? One thing we should never be afraid to do is pause the writing process. To save our work so far, close down the word processor and go back to our notes. If what you're looking for isn't there, then it may be necessary to lapse back into research mode completely. Our mistake, when this happens, is to view this need as a setback. Just because researching a topic doesn't lead to polished words on the page today doesn't mean it's a step backwards. In truth, it is the only logical next step forward.

If you are a fiction writer or a poet and you hit a similar wall, it can be a sign that you have lost touch with the core transformation in your work and the core message you want to convey through the finished product.

Screenwriter Robert McKee has written at some length about the need for a change to take place in every scene of a film. He explains that essentially a change of polarity needs to occur either from positive to negative or from negative to positive. Although to some that might seem quite a reductive view of story structure, I think it's fair to say that a stanza, paragraph or chapter in which nothing changes is less dramatically appealing to a reader. Thus, before sitting down to a piece of writing, it's worth asking ourselves: what journey or change am I trying to show? Cruelty to kindness? Cowardice to bravery? Hatred to love? If you hit a wall while writing, you can then ask yourself what the next step should be in the transformation you are trying to show. What action or conflict brings the speaker or principal character one step closer to their final transformation? Then you can write about that. If you really can't figure out what the next step in that transformation should be – and sometimes we just can't – then think forward in your story or poem to something you can visualise. Is there a scene or moment you can picture happening later on? If so, write that and then, when you've finished, figure out how to get from where you are now to the moment you've just written about. What needs to happen between now and then for the transformation to be rich, vivid and engaging?

In addition to thinking about the transformation at the core of our work, it can also help to think about the reader. How do you want them to feel after they finish reading your last word? What do you think they would like to happen next? How does this fit with the overall message you are trying to convey or theme you are trying to work with? Rather than try and write a polished treatise on this subject, I recommend writing raw in the scrappiest notebook you can find. Give yourself some blank paper and work through some ideas. Reconnect with your purpose. Why are you writing this? What are you trying to show?

Although the above strategies surely won't see you through every eventuality when it comes to hitting a writing block, they will, I hope, at least remind you that it's perfectly OK to give yourself some space from the piece of writing you're working on when you are stuck. Sometimes a change of perspective or a much-needed break can facilitate a transformation in our own thinking, which is usually enough to spur us onward.

CHAPTER 8: GOALS

"I have failed many times, and that is why I am a success." – **Michael Jordan.**

Ever have those days where it feels as though you're never going to fulfil all the goals you've set yourself? I once lived through a time when I experienced many, many days like that as a writer. In such circumstances, we're often quick to berate ourselves. To label ourselves as lazy, or useless, or untalented.

When we experience days like these, we know, deep down, that we are getting something wrong. And we're right about that much. But the thing that's wrong is not our levels of motivation or our resourcefulness or our talent. It is the treatment of ourselves and, perhaps also, our strategy for setting goals.

I see it so often in my classes. Students walk into the room, create some wonderful first draft material and then berate themselves for the fact it is not a polished masterpiece. Though I exhibited the exact same behaviour early in my career, it now still perplexes me when I observe it in others. For who would expect to pick up a guitar and be Jimi Hendrix in the space of ten minutes? Or pick up a paintbrush and be Picasso in the space of an afternoon? When we put it in those terms, it seems ridiculous but perhaps because we have spoken and written in our native language since year dot we are frustrated if we don't see quick progress when we turn around one day and decide that we want to be 'creative'.

As we continue on the journey, our frustration only grows that we cannot write well enough or quick enough. If these feelings persist over the long-term, we will surely abandon a project that had great potential. After all, who wants to spend all their time feeling discouraged and dispirited instead of inspired? Not I.

There is, I'm pleased to say, an alternative to all this. It lies with re-examining our goals. Like everything else, I learnt this the hard way. I was so obsessed with becoming a novelist that anything less than that did not count as 'success' in my eyes. This led to me subconsciously disregarding the many achievements I had in the first ten years of my writing career. I didn't praise myself when I had my first article published in a magazine. I didn't celebrate when the film magazine I founded had been running for a year, or that it went on to run for five years in a time when all other magazines were folding. I told myself that the first non-fiction book I had traditionally published was 'just a coffee table edition' that 'really anyone could have put together' even though it took months to research and compile the photography for that volume.

Naturally, I would never look at the achievements of others this way. This special brand of criticism was reserved only for myself, all of it spoken in that raspy goblin voice. I wasn't keen to acknowledge what my friends and family already understood: I had made it as a writer. Because I hadn't fulfilled my primary goal, all other success was… well, meaningless is a strong word. But let's just say I didn't give myself any credit for it. I was fixated on the fact that I hadn't actualised the one goal some people have to work their entire life for: I hadn't written a novel nor had one published.

As you might gather by the biography at the front of this book, I did eventually get there. And then I got there another time after that, and counting. But out of pure cussedness I did not help myself on the way at all. Worse. I was cruel to myself, belittling whatever achievements I had and categorising them as 'not good enough' or 'not there yet.' It is only now, wizened old writing crone that I am, that I can understand the importance of setting realistic goals, celebrating each milestone and being kind to myself about what I get right. What I DO make happen.

In my experience, we are much more likely to achieve our goals – in any pursuit – if we recognise and acknowledge ourselves for all the steps we take to achieve them along the way. I'm not a runner, and likely never will be, but I imagine an athlete facing a marathon does not focus on the whole twenty-six miles in one go. I imagine they take it one step and one mile at a time. Otherwise, the odds are that it will all just become far too overwhelming.

For example, novelists only tend to commend themselves after they have finished the book. But writing a novel is quite an arduous journey, and this means that measly carrot we're dangling at the end of all the rewrites could be a long time coming. Moreover, many get a third or halfway through writing a book and then have to give up for one reason or another. If we only ever praise ourselves when a project is finished and have cause to give up before it's done, we never get any recognition for the journey. All that work you put into the first third of a book is valuable craft practice and shouldn't be disregarded as a waste of time just because you didn't reach some seemingly untouchable destination.

Consequently, when you set about a writing project I recommend splitting it into small, manageable goals and commending yourself each time you complete one of those tasks. If you recognise the efforts you are putting in on a daily or weekly basis, you are much more likely to reach your end goal. So, in addition to keeping your spirits up, this strategy actually increases the likelihood that you will complete a final, publishable product.

If, for example, your goal is to write a poetry collection, start with one poem. When you have the first draft of that poem, celebrate. That is step one towards a much bigger goal. When you've sent that draft off to an editor, received the feedback and made the revisions, celebrate again. You have your first publishable poem in your hands and have fulfilled this accomplishment of your own accord. Because you wanted to connect with your responsibility as a creator to put good things out into the world rather than sit in front of the television. Not that there's anything wrong with watching TV, I love it. But sometimes I know there are better things I could be doing than rewatching all five seasons of Alias... again. And I take pride in the fact that I chose to create something.

At the time of writing this book, I'm contracted by my publisher to write a novel every six months. If I don't break down the milestones I need to hit in that six-month period it is highly unlikely I'll have a novel finished at the end of it. Consequently, I celebrate after writing the outline for the story. I celebrate after writing the first chapter. I celebrate when I'm 10% into the word count and again at 25% and again at 33% and again at 50% and again at 75% and again at 100% of the raw first draft. Then I celebrate when I have revised it and sent it to my publisher. Then I celebrate when I proofread it after the copy edit. Then I celebrate sending off the final proof. Then I celebrate receiving the final book.

By 'celebrate', what I mean is that I am kind to myself at all points in the journey and acknowledge the work that has gone into a project. Especially given that all the time I'm writing I have no idea how readers might receive it. For all I know, the many days, weeks and months that I spent writing this book might be met with disinterest or disdain. But I still had a go. I still tried to create something, and for that I believe I have a reason to treat myself to a nice meal, a soak in the bathtub with candles, a walk by the canal, a night in with my favourite movie (Die Hard). Whatever celebrating looks like for me at that moment. Since I started doing this, since I started being kind to myself and acknowledging the work I'm putting in, my productivity has skyrocketed.

Thus, when you turn your hand to a creative task, whatever it may be, instead of sitting down and saying to yourself 'I'm going to write my novel/screenplay / poetry collection' why not say to yourself: 'I'm going to write the first five hundred words.' Then, take the time to acknowledge yourself for writing that first five hundred words. Treat yourself. Commend yourself. Be kind to yourself. Those words bring you an important step closer to achieving your big goal.

Focusing on that big goal alone is not likely to bring success and happiness. In part because as soon as you achieve that big goal, the goalpost will move (it has to if you want to continue progressing in a given career). If you do not celebrate and acknowledge your success along the way and the goalposts keep moving, you will wind up feeling as though you have not achieved anything. When, in fact, so long as you are in the process of creating something new, nothing could be further from the truth.

CHAPTER 9: COMPARISONITIS

"A flower does not think of competing with the flower next to it. It Just Blooms." – **Ogui (Sensei).**

Stop comparing yourself to other writers.

I mean it. It is such a waste of your time.

I know it's tempting. When I had my first novel published, I saw the success of all the other novelists working at my imprint and realised I was nowhere near their readership nor sales levels. Only in retrospect do I understand it wasn't a fair comparison. For a start, I did not know how those people had worked themselves into that position in the first place. I was lucky enough to have the first novel that I ever finished published. I subsequently found out one of the other writers published at the same time had written eight novels before she'd had one accepted. She was riding high now but had more than paid her dues in a way that I couldn't even conceive of.

At the same time I was tempted to compare myself, a first-time novelist, with other people who had three, five or even eight books out already. I also looked at the writers who were younger than me and wiled away many an hour agonizing over how much they'd accomplished where I hadn't.

And where did that get me? Absolutely nowhere. Except, maybe several hours behind on starting my next novel. In short, it was wasted time and it was also deeply unfair to my fellow writers who, just like me, were on a journey. Doing their best to muddle through the creative life as best they could.

I have since been on the receiving end of professional jealousy and can tell you it's not a pleasant place to be. When people engage in this, they look only at your success and can be quite mean-spirited, questioning – as if you have the answer - why you, rather than them, should be the one to be picked out of the crowd.

What we cannot see when we are busy comparing ourselves to other people is the sacrifice that led to that success. The highs and lows of the journey they've been on, the difficulties they have faced, the challenges they've overcome and all the time they've spent tapping away on their keyboard rather than lazing in front of the TV. When we compare ourselves and resent others for their good fortune, we reduce them-to what we know of them today, and every person is so much more than that.

Comparison is not only cruel, but fruitless. We are all on different paths. We all start at different places from different viewpoints and with distinct challenges on the road ahead. Some people touch the stars in the first week of their publishing careers, but then the only way is down. Some people will spend years and years writing novel after novel so that they might build their profile and eventually receive just a little recognition for the work they have completed.

We can't possibly know when we start out what our path looks like and the truth is there are as many trails to the mountain-top as there are writers. Although this means there isn't a clear-cut guide to success like there is in, say, real estate, it also means that you can't really get anything 'wrong'. Each trial and each victory is a milestone unique to your journey. And that's the best place for your focus to lie. Other people have their own tracks to follow and will meet their own rocky ground. The Writing Gods (yes, they are a thing, why do you ask?) have not singled you out as the only author who must suffer for your craft. They've just set up your very own unique obstacle course to help you grow as an artist. Yes, they could have made it a little easier on you. Did they have to throw *quite* so much self-doubt into the mix? Probably not. But everyone knows The Writing Gods can be little imps given half a chance. So perhaps, rather than becoming overly-interested in how seemingly well everyone else is doing, we should just do our best to keep our mind on our own affairs and try and meet whatever challenges arise on our own inimitable path to publication.

CHAPTER 10: TAKING FEEDBACK

"There is always space for improvement, no matter how long you've been in the business." **– Oscar De La Hoya.**

How do you handle feedback on your writing?

A polite nod? A neutral 'Hmmm... that's interesting'? A brief but sincere insinuation that you might slash your critic's tyres the second you get out of the workshop?

Receiving feedback on our craft with any measure of grace can be tricky, particularly for beginning writers. The process rubs against two of our most sensitive edges both as writers and as human beings. The first edge is fear. Fear that if we do hand our work over to other people, we might hear some things we don't like about it and then, of course, all of our worst assumptions about our writing talent will be confirmed by a third party. The hobgoblin voice will surely be proven right after all.

Fear can have such a throttlehold on our actions if we don't keep it in check. Particularly when we threaten to step outside of our comfort zone. And handing over our work for critique requires us to do that. It requires us to experience undeniable discomfort.

Because deep down, though we tell people it's 'just a rough draft' and 'we're totally aware of the fact that there are some issues to iron out' what we really long to hear when the work is returned to us is: 'This is the best thing ever written. You are a creative genius.'

Don't try to deny it. I know you hope for it, just like the rest of us.

The sticking point is, while we may want to hear someone commend us for our hard work, we also know that being told we're doing a good enough job without any alteration will not help us develop our skill set. Thus, if we really want to improve, doesn't it make sense to embrace constructive criticism even if it's a little scary to do so?

The truth is, most of the things we truly want are on the other side of fear. If you're considering going through with the somewhat terrifying task of offering your work to other people, I'm assuming that, in this case, what you want more than anything is to become a better writer. You want to develop your craft, and you know you can't do that without feedback.

It is only once we acknowledge this that we realise that being told we're perfect isn't actually what we want to hear at all. Sure, we'd like to hear a little bit about what people are enjoying. After all, there has to be SOMETHING on the page that's worth people's time. A clever simile; an atmospheric description; a line of dialogue that makes people laugh. But if someone told us everything about our work was perfect, we'd be a bit suspicious about that. Certainly, that has been my response when I've been told what I've written can't be bettered. Instead of accepting it, I've sought out others who I thought might be much harsher critics and essentially forced them to find a few things that don't add up about my work. Maybe that wasn't necessary but I hold myself to a high standard and, I think, if we want to be taken seriously as writers holding ourselves to a high standard is one of the best ways of achieving that.

What we really need and want to hear when we submit our work for critique then is not that we have produced perfection. But that there are some avenues we could explore to enrich the work to even greater effect. Even if everything is sort of working just fine at a basic level. We want to do our best and we can't do that without receiving some frank feedback so, in essence, accepting the fear and discomfort of that process is the price we pay for becoming better at something we love. I'm OK with that price. I've paid it many times over and every single time it has been worth it. Nothing in this world comes without a cost attached to it and by becoming part of the writer community, you are tacitly agreeing to paying the price of some occasional fear and discomfort in order to improve. I promise you, the world won't end over it. So why worry?

Remember before, back I got super-philosophical, I said there were two edges that this process rubs against? The second is vulnerability. Submitting our work for feedback demands a profound level of vulnerability from us, and that often takes us full circle back to fear. We live in a world where it is increasingly difficult to be vulnerable. In education and business, making a mistake is held up as the worst thing you can do. We therefore take fewer risks - such as handing over our work to people when we don't know what they'll say about it.

The more you can embrace your vulnerability, however, the more successful you will be in connecting with readers and improving your writing craft. When it comes to how we learn, making mistakes is a crucial part of the journey. It's very difficult to learn anything without making mistakes. So how about just accepting them? Making peace with the fact that your raw first draft is going to have mistakes in it and that, when you ask them to, people will point them out in the spirit of helping you do better.

The fact that your first draft is imperfect doesn't mean *you* are imperfect. It doesn't make you a terrible writer. It doesn't mean you should give up. It just means you are like the rest of us: you have strengths you're proud of and areas where you can improve.

Thus, all in all, I recommend you make gratitude your starting point when accepting critical feedback on your work. After all, what you're being offered here is an opportunity to improve on something that is extremely important to you. Somebody else has taken the time to read your work and make some recommendations on how to make it better. That is a gift, any way you look at it. So even if you don't agree with it all, and the likelihood of you agreeing with it all is vanishingly small, just say 'thank you'.

Do not start an impassioned defence of the creative choices that have been picked at. Do not tell the other person that you think they're wrong and you won't be making any of their suggested changes, thank-you-very-much. If you're in a workshop setting, do not pull apart your critic's piece of writing just because they critiqued your work. Leave with your dignity intact and simply ruminate on the suggestions you've been offered. There's no rule to say that you have to accept what they have told you as gospel. But isn't it worth keeping an open mind and exploring one or two of the possibilities? Surely it's best to do explore them now before your work is in front of hundreds, possibly thousands, of readers who might not be so kind when giving their opinion on what you've created?

Alongside showing gratitude for the opportunity to improve, it's also often prudent to exercise some control over the kind of feedback you receive. If you're in a workshop setting, the workshop facilitator should give you the opportunity to explain what kind of feedback would be helpful. You shouldn't feel shy about asking for only positive feedback on your work. This isn't the cop out it might sound. It could be that you're at the very early stages of your work and just want to know if you're on the right track. So ask people in your workshop group, or a hired editor, to only comment on the things that are working so far.

Finding out what people enjoy about your work gives you an opportunity to put more of that stuff in there. Additionally, you can, by process of elimination, figure out some of the elements you might need to work on without having to run the gauntlet of critical feedback while the project is still in its infancy. If all the positive comments you receive are on characterisation and setting, it might be that you would do well to look at the structure of your writing. Is your story getting started at the most dramatic moment? Are you clear on the journey your central character is taking chapter by chapter? Stanza by stanza? Scene by scene? If all your comments are about the structure, you could likewise go back to your work on the second pass and double check your characterisation and setting are vivid.

If you are ready to move a step beyond this, you could ask for feedback on what is clear and what is unclear. This again focuses the feedback in a way that is most helpful to you and prevents people, particularly in a workshop setting, from hijacking your work and responding with a clear agenda of their own which may not be your key consideration as an author.

You could even get a great deal more granular than what I have described above. When we have a 'difficult' workshop experience, it can sometimes be a product of the idea that writers have to sit passively through the experience and just take whatever is dished out. Your facilitator may have a rule that you don't speak while your work is being discussed – this isn't to silence you, but to ensure you are listening rather than launching into a defence of your work. Before the discussion starts, however, you are very much within your rights to stipulate specific areas of your work that you would like to be critiqued. Be that characterisation, dialogue, pacing or any other aspect of the extract you are concerned about. That way, if anyone starts talking about something else, you can politely remind them that today you are only interested in feedback on your chosen topic.

Besides helping you focus your revisions, this strategy prevents the workshop environment from becoming a 'free for all'. This, of course, shouldn't happen if you have a facilitator who has carefully structured the workshop but in my time teaching creative writing I'm sorry to say I have heard some horror stories. So, just in case, always be prepared to set your own boundaries.

Perhaps the last point to touch upon when it comes to constructive criticism is what to do with it once you have it. Regardless of what kind of feedback you receive from fellow writers and editors, never forget that you are the author of the work and have the final say on all changes. So, claim that space, give yourself some time apart from the manuscript, come back with a clear head and decide which things you agree with and which you do not.

When Neil Gaiman wrote his now-famous eight rules for writers, he slipped one into fifth position that I think is always worth consideration when deliberating feedback:

"Remember: when people tell you something's wrong or doesn't work for them, they are almost always right. When they tell you exactly what they think is wrong and how to fix it, they are almost always wrong."

From Gaiman's perspective, people are often good at spotting problems but not that great at coming up with a solution, and I have to admit that has also been my experience. Other writers can usually spot when something doesn't feel right, but any suggested fixes aren't usually in your voice or in keeping with your vision. Thus, the best thing you can do is look for consensus in the comments you receive. Has more than one person picked on the same moment as problematic? If so, think about how you could smooth things over for the reader so that the problem they've picked out is no longer evident. The odds are if it's annoyed more than one reader in a workshop setting, it will also annoy readers in a more general sense. So take a look. Doctor it where you can, and move on with gratitude in your heart for those people who helped you look a little bit smarter and more articulate in front of the book-devouring masses.

CHAPTER 11: BEWARE ABSOLUTES

"An attempt can be a failure, a person never is." **Brad Brown.**

The most frequent fear expressed by writers I talk to, work with and tweet at, is a fear of inadequacy. That what they've written is subpar. That they are subpar. And isn't that something we hear a lot from the voice in our head? That, one way or another, we're just not good enough.

Like at 3am when you're wide awake. Mulling over that ending you wrote a few hours ago. Something about it just isn't quite right. Oh and, while we're on the subject of stuff that isn't quite right, that crooked tooth you have. The one at the front. You tell yourself it's cute, and sort of endearing, but it's really just crooked and that's that.

Sorry.

In the cold depths of the early hours, that little goblin voice takes no prisoners. It deals in absolutes; in terms of always and never.

You'll always be a failure.

You'll never make it.

And those stark assertions sound pretty convincing, don't they? There's just one problem: both statements refer to the future. And yellow-fanged little goblins can't tell the future any better than we can. Thus, those statements are unverifiable, most likely false. In fact, these ideas only have power in the present if you believe them because that will probably lead to lower productivity and lower effort on your part. If you don't believe in yourself, it will make it much, much harder to get anyone else to.

So, don't let the goblin voice trick you on this. If you're telling yourself something – anything – negative about the future, you can't possibly know if that's really going to happen for sure. So why not give yourself the best chance of a good outcome by thinking positive? Or, at the very least, remaining neutral on the subject.

Occasionally your goblin voice will use a different tack. Still working with absolutes but using the present tense:

You always write rubbish.

You never write anything worth a damn.

Always and never are still in the mix, but this time the criticism is not attached to future outcomes but to your current levels of achievement. This switch to the now, however, only makes it easier to disprove the goblin's theory.

You *always* write rubbish.

Excuse me? *Always?* Not possible. The law of averages is strongly against that. Not every little thing that comes out my pen can be rubbish, always. That would sort of be a strange talent unto itself. At some point, if only by accident, I will write a half-decent simile. Probability is on my side on that one. Sorry yellow fangs, tell your story walking.

I know, I know. You want to achieve more than writing a half-decent simile once in a while. And what if you don't have the natural talent to make that happen? Are you wasting your time? Is the goblin voice right?

No.

Look, I'll level with you. I'm a straight-talking northern lass; it's the way I live.

There are some people out there who have natural writing talent. But are they the only people in the world writing? Of course not. Are they the only people in the world who are decent at writing? No. They have a fortunate leg-up. A head-start. Nothing more. If writing doesn't come naturally, then maybe you won't become The Greatest Writer Of All Time ™ but, so what? Does that mean you should give up? That you can't seduce readers into a story? Or move people?

For most of us, writing is a craft that takes hours and hours of practice. On the whole, once people commit to it, writing becomes a lifelong pursuit. One you will still be learning until the day you finally die in some comical, but strangely predicable, piano-on-the-head incident.

However good or bad your writing is today, it's important to recognise it for what it is: an attempt at creating something. That attempt *might* be a failure in *some* respects. But that attempt is not you or the full picture when it comes to your writing abilities. And today is not forever. Tomorrow you get to make another attempt and see what happens. But only if you keep trying. If you give up, if you let the little goblin voice win because its lies seem convincing, then you will never know what you could have achieved.

Sure, modesty is healthy. And arrogance is indeed an unpalatable character trait but there's a difference between humility and belittling yourself.

So if it brings you joy to do so, please keep writing. No matter what the goblin says, keep writing and keep trying. Keep making new attempts. Write every day. Write a word. A sentence. A joke. A love-note. Write nonsense in your diary and photograph it for a blog post. But most importantly, write.

The only thing you owe yourself, or anyone else, is to be the best you can be today. If. for any reason, the work isn't quite where you want it to be then tomorrow you will have the opportunity to come back to it, edit it, knead the words into place and, trust me, when it's finally out there nobody who reads it will suspect a thing.

CHAPTER 12: THE END?

"There is no real ending. It's just the place where you stop the story." **– Frank Herbert.**

How do you know when a piece of work is finished?

This is one of the most common questions I am asked by other writers. For reasons I'm not quite sure of, they seem to think I am privy to some kind of objective benchmarking criteria that, when met, allows a writer to send their work off to the publisher or editor with confidence in its quality.

You can likely imagine their distaste when I tell them that their work will most definitely be published before it is perfect. If I, or any other writer, waited around for perfection, there wouldn't be many books in the world. The truth is that most writers who have work published would be able to point out a thousand niggling little corrections they would like to make to their projects in hindsight. Certainly I feel that way about every book I write. Especially as my craft has developed with each book I've written.

My first three novels received wonderful reviews from all over the world, but I'm the first to admit that they were not perfect. Still, I am immensely proud of those books because they represent the best I could do at that time. They are markers on a journey that I have taken through this craft and when I see the little things I did then that I know better than to do now, I smile and am grateful that there are still things to learn fifteen years into my professional writing journey. I hope that there will still be things to learn right up until the day I die.

With this in mind, I advise other writers to focus on delivering the best work you can today rather than fixating on some untouchable, unobtainable perfection. I then suggest a process which I will share with you now that, I believe, gives you the best chance of ensuring quality control when you send work out into the world.

The first step is to write the first draft as a writer, not an editor. When you write the first draft of anything, be it a poem, a script, a novel or a short story, you are best served by staying in that experimental, playful space of the writer. Far from the judgmental eye of your inner editor. That part of you will come in handy later, but not at the point of creation. You need to be open to every possible idea. You can quality assess the ideas later. But for now let yourself be surprised by your own ingenuity; your own sensitivity; your whimsical streak that you tether in, let those parts of you run riot.

Have fun.

Once you have your first draft, put it away. Do not look at it for as long as you can stand, but at the very least give it a fortnight. Work on other projects; write daily pages; keep a journal; write some letters but don't look at that work.

When the time is up, take it from its hiding place and read it as though you were reading the work of a friend you want to help with their writing. Be kind, honest but kind, and ask yourself: what is clear and what is unclear?

It is perfectly fine for plenty of things to be unclear at this stage. There is no need to berate yourself. This was a raw first draft for your eyes only. You were experimenting. You were getting the story straight in your own head and now with your editor's eye you can kindly tell the friend you are trying to help which parts make sense to you and which confuse you. Then you can try and fix them. By the simple act of making your work clear you will be a head of hundreds of writers who are so close to the story they can't tell you what is clear and what is not.

Read your work again. This time look for any instances where you are showing off to the reader. You know what I mean; I do it too. I use an eight syllable word where a two syllable word will do. I drop in some obscure mythical or literary reference that lets the reader know that, even though I didn't get the best grades at school, I am smart.

OK, maybe you're a better person than me and you don't do this on your first draft but I see it in a lot of work that I edit so I know I'm not alone. And it's OK that we fell into the trap of putting ourselves before the reader because this was our first draft. OURS.

This one was for us; for the pleasure and the joy of it. But if we want to show it to readers we have to make sure that they can access it. So, re-read your work and check that it is accessible to your target reader. Is there anything that might trip them up? Anything that might make them put the book down because in my own efforts to look smart I accidentally made the reader feel stupid?

Once you've ironed out all of the above, do one last pass. This time to check accuracy. Sometimes accuracy is not relevant to a piece of work. For example, a poem doesn't actually have to accurately follow the rules of science or nature if it is whimsical or experimental. But where applicable, check your facts. Have you got the details of the setting, dialect, the historical aspects, the logical aspects, the spellings of important places and people correct? Look at this now before anyone else sees your work and if you catch any typographical errors, spelling errors or grammar errors along the way, even better.

By now you've taken three passes at your work it's about as shipshape as you're going to get it on your own. This means that it's time to pass it on to other readers. Perhaps you have a trusted reader or you're part of a workshop group. Alternatively, you might have a trusted editor you hire as a freelancer. Whoever it is, hand your work over to them and explain what kind of feedback you think you need. If you're handing it to more than one person look for consensus in their feedback. If all three readers pick on one thing that really irritates them or makes little sense to them, you need to revisit that point in your work and reassess what you have written with their comments in mind.

With an editor you see eye-to-eye with, you will probably act on eighty percent of their comments and then use authorial judgement with the other twenty percent. In these instances, you may opt to do something other than what the editor has suggested or opt not to make any alteration at all.

Once you've finished all the editorial changes, give the piece of work one last proof.

If you follow these steps, then your writing is ready to be out there. If you are particularly concerned about your grammar, you may also choose to hire a copy-editor to do a line edit for you. But after this you can confidently send your work to agents, publishers, magazines and competitions knowing that you will have quality assessed your work to a standard most other people will not have done. Some might say this is all a lot of effort, and it is. But if you are going to send something out into the world with your name on it, surely quality assessing that work is worth your time? If you are entering competitions and submitting to publications on which your literary reputation is going to be built, that time and money investment is going to pay off in the future at some point. And all the steps outlined above increase the likelihood of that payoff happening sooner rather than later. By following this process, you amplify your chances of acceptance, which means you will not likely have to spend as much time going back and forward with publications, getting rejected left, right and centre, damaging your self-esteem and failing to move forward in your career. All things that, I think you'll agree, we'd all sooner avoid if we could.

CHAPTER 13: HANDLING REJECTION

"If you live for people's acceptance, you will die from their rejection." – **Lecrae.**

In October 2015, I spent an entire afternoon of my life lying in the fetal position on our living room floor. I didn't even have the strength to cry at that point. I was just lying there, being depressed, because I received yet another rejection email from yet another agent on a book that, as far as I could tell, was well-written and was aimed at a clear audience.

Just a month later I would receive an email from Harper Collins explaining they wanted to publish my book. But I didn't know that then. I let the sly, deceitful narrator at the back of my mind who always came out when my creative projects didn't go to plan fool me into wasting valuable creation time by lying, like a baby, on the floor for a whole afternoon at the age of thirty-four.

Is it embarrassing to admit this?

Yes.

I would much rather not tell you about that afternoon. It represents one of the lowest points in my creative career. It transpired simply because I had failed to find a publishing professional who could verify that my work was worth something. At that moment, I believed it wasn't. And because I am a writer before anything else I felt that if my writing wasn't worth anything, then *I* wasn't worth anything.

My poor husband got a bit of a start when he came home from the office that day. At that time he was studying for his PhD, and frankly had other things on his plate to deal with besides his unemployed, writer-of-wife falling to pieces on the living room floor. To his credit, he offered me tea and sympathy. Not literally. I don't drink tea. But I'm sure some kind of soothing beverage was involved. He didn't really know what to say to me. I didn't really know what to say to him, or myself. I'd hit a wall, and I just didn't know how to break through it. Honestly, I didn't know if I had the strength to.

I'm sharing this deeply embarrassing story because I think, if you take your writing seriously, you've probably had an afternoon like the one I spent on the living room floor. I'm not suggesting that you would be dramatic enough to let your feelings manifest in quite the same way I did. You've probably got a great deal more common sense than to be rolling around on the floor without good reason. But I believe you will have experienced similar knockbacks; similar setbacks; similar feelings, similar self-doubt and despair, and you probably found your own unique way of working through those feelings.

You too have probably got to the point when you ask yourself: is my writing worth anything? Am *I* worth anything? In short, you've probably got to the point of asking yourself: why should I bother? What's the point if nobody takes notice? It's like that old proverb about a tree falling in the forest: if nobody hears it fall, did it really fall? If nobody reads your work, are you really writing anything?

After this questionable reaction to a rejection email, I knew I had to do some deep reflection on my approach to creative projects. I had self-published books in the past and had revelled in not having to ask anyone's permission to put my non-fiction workout in the world. For some reason, when it came to my fiction, I was hell-bent on getting somebody else's approval. For some reason, I needed external validation to certify that both me and my work were good enough.

Why? Why did I need that when I had already written so much by that point and had plenty of articles published in magazines, journals and websites? Why was I here, playing a game of cat and mouse with publishers and agents? I don't mind admitting to you, in the spirit of honesty, that, for me, the need for validation goes back to my parents. I love my parents very much. They love me very much. But they were not big champions of my choice to be a writer in the beginning. You've heard about this in earlier chapters. You know why they felt the way they felt. But the subconscious is a tricky place and somewhere deep down I still needed somebody else to tell me that my work, and by extension that I, was good enough.

My reaction to that rejection email was disproportionate to say the least. It echoed how *badly* I wanted that validation. If I was living in the 19th century and traditional publishers were my only real route to finding a readership, then perhaps I might have been justified to be upset by that rejection. But I am living in the 21st Century when the miracle of the internet is available and numerous self-publishing platforms are there to be exploited. If I genuinely, hand-on-heart, only care about getting my stories out into the world, why do I, a grown woman, need somebody else to give me permission? The answer is: I do not.

After that fateful day, I decided that if a publisher was not forthcoming, I would put the book out into the world myself. Other people might not have seen it as anything grander than a light-hearted genre read but I was proud of it and wanted to get it into the hands of readers. Even if I had to do that bit myself.

Then, much like buses, sexual partners and almost anything else that one might actively seek in this world, the moment I wasn't looking for a publisher, one came knocking.

I took a couple of different lessons away from that dark afternoon on the living room floor. The first was that no matter how bleak things look in the moment, you never know what is going to happen in your life next. If you continue to put your work out there, it has a higher chance of landing on the right desk.

When I teach this principle in my creative writing classes, I often dish out some fragments of sea glass; little shards from broken bottles, vases and other spilled cargo that have been slowly weathered over the years by the ocean. Because I'm a nature nerd on top of everything else – I know I just keep getting cooler – I collect sea glass, pebbles and shells They are my own version of sea treasure and I can spend many a merry hour at the shoreline combing for what other people regard as worthless shrapnel. The reason I hand sea glass out to my class is not to apprise them of my strange, and perhaps somewhat sad, hobbies but to physically demonstrate a core principle of writing practice. Sea glass, a largely underappreciated commodity, becomes a thing of subtle beauty that brings joy to me and fellow sea glass collectors (yes, there is more than one of us, make your peace with it) when tossed and turned by the ocean for several years.

We are like the sea glass. Some days we are going to rest in shallow, calm pools, other days we will be washed to new horizons and sometimes we will be caught up in a storm that we do not think we can possibly survive. Arguably, however, pushing through the struggle to find peace again leads us to become even more beautiful, more valued. The same is true of our writing. An editor might disregard it today. But if we turn our writing over and over as the tide does the sea glass, eventually it becomes smoother, polished and desirable.

The second lesson that I learnt from that afternoon was really a reminder of something I already understood: that it is unwise to pin your esteem on the subjective opinion of another human being. I vowed that was the last rejection letter that was ever going to hit me hard, and it's a promise I've kept.

For if a rejection does hit us unduly hard, it is wise to ask why. Why do we need somebody else to approve of what we have written so badly? The answer rarely has anything to do with your craft and if you are brave enough to explore the answer you have the opportunity disconnect your craft from a more general need for validation.

Nobody should be lying on their living room floor rocking from side-to-side over a rejection email. And, in truth, I wasn't. I was lying on the living room floor because I didn't feel like enough. As soon as I reminded myself that I was, I could dust myself off and continue on. But I couldn't do that before I had acknowledged that what stood in my way was not the approval of other people but my own approval of myself.

Entwined in these strange thoughts and feelings was my inability to differentiate between my writing and myself. I had also temporarily lost the ability to differentiate between an attempt and the big picture where my writing is concerned. If I write something today which is rejected it doesn't mean that my writing is bad. Or that all writing in the future will be will be rejected. As discussed in previous chapters, with every day and every page, I have a fresh opportunity to try again.

It's particularly important to remember this when the person looking at my work might reject it for some arbitrary reason that has nothing to do with the general quality of the piece and that I couldn't possibly conceive of. Factors such as: they don't like stories set in America. They're looking for stories set in Europe or the Far East. Or maybe they commissioned a book just like mine last week or are not confident they can sell it to the readership they have built. None of these reasons mean my book is terrible, that my work is unreadable or that I am a dreadful writer.

You can be sure that's what your mind will try and convince you of, but it is imperative that you catch it in the lie and instead focus on the truth: the writing is journey one you have committed to. Some days going will be easy and during others you will find bumps in the road. But the only alternative to this road is one where you do not write. If you do not want to travel *that* road, then the best thing you can do is keep believing in your own work. Be your own champion and remember that the only approval that really matters when it comes to putting your work out there is your own.

Though rejection can feel painfully personal, the truth is that it's numbers game. Getting published, at least via the traditional route, is largely about getting your work on the right desk. You need to find a way of putting it in front of that person who says 'yes' because they believe they can sell what you've produced. You may or may not achieve that straight away. If you find a particular piece is being rejected over and over this simply might not be the correct time for it in the traditional market. In which case you might decide to do something with that piece of work yourself such as self-publish it on your blog via a self-publishing platform, send it into a competition or look at crowdfunding options such as Patreon.

Yes, this will require you to perhaps redefine your idea of what it means to be 'published' but the world of independent publishing is no longer the Ugly Sister of the traditional route. Independent authors are hitting the best-seller lists, winning awards and selling books in their millions. I'm an independently published author (heck, you are currently reading one of my independently published books). I was independently published when I landed my first traditional book deal and it didn't hurt my career even a little bit. In fact, if anything it helped because the publisher knew I already understood what it meant to finish and put together a saleable book.

The independent route isn't for everyone however (I talk more about the pros and cons of traditional and independent publishing in my book *How & When to Sign a Book Deal*). Consequently, you might decide to bank that manuscript until it is the right time, put it in a drawer and hope to sell it later. Even in the face of rejection however, you have choices. Particularly if you remember that persistence is key. If you refuse to give up on finding the people who will enjoy your work, be they readers, agents or editors, very little can stand in your way of becoming a published writer.

CHAPTER 14: COMPLETION

It is almost a guarantee that about a third of the way through a writing project some new, exciting idea will start flashing its shoulder at you. Luring you, like a siren, from the commitment you have already made to your current work in progress. Daring you to throw away all that hard work and, instead, start courting this seemingly sassier, slinkier story concept, which is so full of untouched possibilities.

This kind of temptation is tough to ignore. Your heart rat rises as you experience again that feeling of being kissed for the first time by a new idea. It's so much younger and hotter than the idea you're currently wedded to, the reality of which is nice enough but you can't help but wonder if there is more out there for you. If you push your current project aside in favour of this new, sparkling proposition surely there will be more surprises? More excitement? More potential?

And then we wake from our trance, pour ourselves a cup of tea, and wonder why we never get anything finished.

When this inevitably happens, do yourself a favour: write the idea down. Spend a whole damn afternoon writing about it if you want. But just the gist. Just the outline. Just the bare bones and then lock it safely away in a folder marked 'Future Projects.' Alternatively, get a bit promiscuous and divide your writing time equally between the two projects, working on them in tandem. But please, don't give up on your current project. If we never commit fully to an idea and see it through to its fruition, the simple truth stands that we will never finish anything.

Completion is a huge deal for writers. This singular sticking point is one of the key reasons so very few people finish a manuscript and even fewer have their work traditionally published. Lots of people *start* writing a poem, a short story, a script or a novel but never finish the job. And the harsh reality is that if something never gets finished, it can never be published.

I have some experience in this area.

Yes, I did get the first novel I ever *finished* published by Harper Collins. But that wasn't the first novel I ever *started*. There were numerous discarded stories over the years that never made it past the first few pages. There was also the big literary masterpiece I was going to write. Remember that from the chapter on goal setting? The first time I tried to write a novel I got about halfway through, had a big falling out with my chief character and parted ways with the project. I don't regret leaving behind that old idea because I knew in my heart of hearts I had taken it as far as I could. But you should know I didn't give up without a fight. Sure the fight was just with myself, but I wanted to be sure I had done all I could to hold on to that project because I had got further with it than I had any other story I had written before.

Ultimately, however, I knew it was wasn't going to work out. The same way you know when you're in a dissatisfying relationship but don't really want to rock the boat because you share a lease on a property and will have to divide your record collection. So I'm not saying you should never give up on a project but I am recommending that you shouldn't give up without a fight, without being one hundred percent sure that you've done all you can to save it – not just because a new idea comes knocking. If you keep this rule, then when you do walk away from twenty thousand, fifty thousand, or maybe even seventy thousand words, at least you will know you did everything in your power to make it work first.

After my first big break-up with a protagonist, it was another four years before I started another novel. Once I had finished that one, I had the confidence that I could do it again – which I did. And have done it six times over at the time of writing this book. In that time I have noticed that I tend to get my head turned by another idea about a third of the way through the writing of every book I start. The distraction comes just when things are getting sticky and I have to figure out plot points that weren't in my original outline. In short, they appear when I have to do some proper work to make things move forward.

Only with experience have I learned that when such a new idea starts winking at me, it isn't really the idea that I find tantalizing.

I'm lured by some projected, idealistic meditation of my greatest possible potential. *If I just had the right idea*, my inner goblin muses, *I could be so much better than this*. Instead of truly hearing those words, however, when this thought process surfaces, I now hear a warning klaxon. The goblin voice is trying to trick me again. Trying to get me to give up. Trying to make sure I never complete anything so I can avoid all the rejection and scrutiny. Because the goblin voice believes that is too high a toll to pay for crossing the bridge and becoming a published writer. On that however, and much else, we disagree. Which is why I keep writing and finish my work. Unless we do that, our chances of publication plummet to zero, and, oh, how the goblin cackles when he wins.

CHAPTER 15: HANDLING BAD REVIEWS

"Just smile sweetly and suggest - as politely as you possibly can - that they go make their own fucking art. Then stubbornly continue making yours." – **Elizabeth Gilbert.**

My dream response to the question 'how do you handle bad reviews?' would be to say 'I couldn't possibly know how to handle a bad review because I've never received one.'

But I'm not a liar.

I've totally received plenty of bad reviews. Mostly from people who feel it's their right, nay, their duty to tear apart what was supposed to be a gentle murder mystery yarn to help people wile away a Saturday afternoon when there's nothing on TV. Which is most Saturday afternoons, am I right?

Some small part of me (the part that is still living in 1999 and listening to Eminem) believes that I could buy some much-needed street credibility with you, dear reader if I told you I handled bad reviews by drinking a bottle of wine. In truth, I'm a mere 5'4 and if I drank a bottle of wine you'd have to take me to hospital. So that's out and, let's face it, it's not exactly the healthiest response to this issue.

Allow me to offer some alternatives.

My first brush with reviewers came in 2010 when I decided to start a film magazine which I, masochistically, edited on top of a full-time teaching job. I was super-proud of that project. Partly because it was something that almost everyone with a set of working vocal cords said I couldn't do. The publication ran for five years and all told it was a hard learning curve. I made all of my mistakes publicly in black and white. Once the issue had gone to press, there was no taking it back. No re-editing. No pretending that wasn't the final draft.

As a woman who dared to think she could establish a magazine in a male-dominated arena, some of the feedback I received, though by no means all of it, was scathing. When this happened, I don't mind telling you, I was gutted. I would think to myself: all that work, and all these people can focus on is a couple of typos. Or that the design isn't quite to their liking.

When I think back to how I felt in those moments, it is unsurprising to me that one of the most frequent questions asked in my creative writing classes is how to manage, digest and generally cope with criticism and bad reviews. I try not to take it too personally that my students think I would have a lot of experience in dealing with this issue. Joking apart, this is a challenge pretty much every writer on the planet has to address at some point and is thus more than worthy of acknowledgment.

If you think some writers might be immune, visit an online bookstore at your next opportunity and find your favourite book. The book that changed your life. The book that made you love a particular genre. The book that you've read over and over again. If you're a writer I'm assuming you have one, most writers do. While online, go to the reviews section and filter out the one or two star ratings. Even a very well-reviewed book will have criticisms within those reviews. Take a look at some of them. Get angry. Wonder why some people don't see genius when it's right in front of them. You did, after all, just decide that this book was your favourite out of all the books and some anonymous web user has gone out of their way to trash it.

In case you're wondering, I don't get my kicks by asking people to acknowledge how terribly reviewers treat their favourite books. That's right, you thought I was just being mean because we're almost at the end of the book and you're expecting some kind of twist where I show my true colours and reveal some insidious agenda. But as it turns out, being insidious is quite time-consuming, and I asked you to read the hack-job reviews of your favourite books because I have a point. By engaging in this process, you develop a deeper understanding of the fact that even a person you would hold up as a literary great is subject to criticism. Consequently, when you are criticized or receive poor reviews, at least you will know you are not alone and, in fact, are in the same club as your favourite author.

What kind of reviews can you expect that would be classed in the negative bracket? First of all, you need to prepare yourself for the fact that some readers will hate your work for some completely capricious reason. Because your protagonist wears a hat; because they didn't want to know what colour the curtains were in your main character's house or because they decide the title or the cover is not an exact match for the story you've written.

Readers will also get angry at you for using well-established genre tropes even though the majority of your readers will expect you to use them. I can't tell you, as the author of a murder mysteries, how many times I've read in a review: 'this character has no business investigating this murder' it's almost as if these people have never seen an episode of *Murder She Wrote* or read a single Miss Marple story.

When I read reviews like this, I can't help but giggle. I know I'm supposed to take critical reviews of my work more seriously than that, but what can I tell you? Life is short, and it seems pointless to get hung up on the fact that a reader is unfamiliar with my genre. Or perhaps even storytelling itself. For if my characters minded their own business and followed all the rules, there would be no story.

I just have to accept that I'm not going to please absolutely everybody. Seriously, it's an impossible task and if you try to hold yourself to that you are likely to go quite mad. Some readers will be big fans of the genre you're writing in. Others might be drawn in by the cover or the blurb and choose to take a punt and read outside their genre. Others may be part of an online product review service in which they were rating a new line in air fresheners yesterday and your novel today. I have no need, nor desire, to please everyone on this list. Sure, if someone takes a punt on my book I hope they like it but it simply can't be to everyone's tastes because tastes are so varied.

Thus, instead of focusing on the people you can't please, it makes more sense to focus on the people you are pleasing. Hopefully, you will verify the existence of at least a few such individuals through your book sales page, your blog or via social media. Moreover, it's important to never forget the existence of the silent majority.

While attending a publishing conference in early 2020, I had the privilege of watching independent author LJ Ross speak about her experience of publishing and writing murder mysteries. She explained that when you write a book, you often hear from two different people: those that really loved it and those that really hated it. But somewhere between these two extremes are the people you never hear from. The people who enjoyed your book just fine. While these people will buy your next book without hesitation, they don't post to your Amazon page or send you an email. These non-vocal followers show their allegiance to your work through their ongoing commitment to buying your books. Ultimately, your goal is to reach a wide readership and as such you will reach many people who perhaps aren't your biggest fans on the planet but really like what you do. With this in mind, it is unwise to get too fixated on the reviews you receive as they are likely to be the most extreme reactions, one way or the other, to your work. Somewhere in the middle hundreds, maybe thousands, of people are finding your books enjoyable.

If you receive a lot of the same critical feedback from readers however, or if your sales never really take off, it could be that something was missed in your manuscript. Something that, if fixed, could have improved the overall product. Nobody likes to be told that their best isn't good enough but if you find this out and it is too late to fix it, please do not despair. Remember what I wrote about seeking perfection? It doesn't exist. We might get close but often we will miss the mark because while we are writing and publishing we are also learning. In circumstances where it becomes apparent you shot wide of one mark or another, it's important to be humble enough to learn any necessary lessons. If you are truly planning to make a career out of being a writer, you will likely be writing in the long-term. This means you may make some mistakes in your early books, which you then try and rectify in your later books. Lots of authors do this. It's no big deal.

Having the first novel I finished picked up for publication was, of course, cause for glorious celebration, but it has also meant that I refined and honed my craft in the public sphere, with everybody watching. If I could go back and rewrite or edit certain portions of the books I have written now I'd be very tempted. Yes, despite what I've written in earlier chapters I am just as susceptible as anyone else to the idea of creating 'perfection'. Even if I have to do it retroactively. But the truth is those books are the best I could do at the time. They were accepted for publication and, on the whole, the people who read them enjoyed them and continue to buy my work.

Do I think I'm a more seasoned writer now on novel six then I was on novel one? Yes. If that wasn't the case, I would be worried. If I was never going to get any better no matter how many words I wrote then that would be a point of sadness for me. And yes, there have been reviewers who have pointed out the flaws and blemishes in my work but most people have forgiven the slight errors as they have enjoyed the bigger elements of the story too much to notice.

Ultimately, writing prose, scripts and poetry collections is a public journey and, as such, I'm afraid it's just a fact of life that some people will point and jeer. Others will actually go out of their way to trip you up. But they will be the minority and regardless of what such people say about what you have produced remember this, and never forget it: you wrote a book, they didn't. You created something; they stood on the side-lines. You took the hard and meaningful path; they took the quick and easy path. For it is always, *always* more difficult to create something than it is to criticise. This is something that tall writers and artists of all walks understand, and it is a truth that you would do well to hold close to your heart whenever you are facing the disturbing netherworld of the Amazon review box.

CHAPTER 16: MOVING ON

Over the course of this book I have explored various elements of becoming a published writer that seem to cause the most consternation amongst the practitioners I've come into contact with. But the truth is, no matter how much we refine them or whereabouts we are in our writing career, not every piece of work will find a place with a traditional publisher.

Within these pages, I've touched upon several other avenues you can explore with a piece of writing when that happens. Avenues that negate the need for a traditional publisher. But if your heart is set solely and completely on traditional publishers, it is very important that you learn to let go and move on when the time is clearly not right for the manuscript you have created. If you don't do this, it could mean the end of your writing career. Or at the very least a long hiatus.

Amongst the many random day jobs I took on during my twenties was a position as a bid writer for a national logistics and facilities company. My direct boss was a lovely chap and, like so many who spend their days writing business copy of some nature, he had aspirations of becoming a novelist. I told him I shared the same dream but, before I could ask him more about his book, he shut the subject down. He had sent his manuscript out to every agent he could find and they had all said no. The experience, he explained, had destroyed any hope he had of getting published and he was very straight up about the fact that he wasn't ever going to try again.

At this point, I hadn't even started the novel I would abandon. I knew nothing about the world of publishing. But even then, as he relayed his story, I thought to myself, 'what a shame'. What a shame that this one big knock-back meant that he wouldn't keep writing, wouldn't keep trying. I could tell from his tone that he considered the piece he'd written to be a serious literary endeavour, so it wasn't like I could suggest he might write a silly spy thriller just for the fun of it and see if he felt better again. Who was I to advise him anyway when I had no frame of reference whatsoever?

Knowing what I know now, even though he might not have enjoyed hearing it, I wish I had taken a punt and advised him to have some fun on the page anyway. My position there was only temporary, so I have no idea if he ever did write anything else. I hope so, because if anything at all has come across throughout the reading of this book I hope it is that your life and career do not hang by the success or failure of one piece of writing.

It's fine to want to stick with the traditional method of publishing if that is really what's in your heart, but once you have exhausted all of those possibilities, have the courage and the grace to tuck that manuscript away for a later date and soldier onward into new horizons. Holding on to something too long is one of the most restrictive things we can do both as writers and human beings. So if you have no luck this time, trust that you might in the future and write something else.

If you do not shift your focus onto something new, there's a risk of becoming obsessed with the success or failure of one piece of work. That is not going to do your self-esteem any good. It's also not going to help your productivity levels. Do not fall into the trap of believing that this one piece of work is the only thing you will ever produce of worth. The odds are strongly, strongly against that.

Even when you do get a piece of work published, don't dwell. Don't spend all your time harassing the publisher asking for updates. Sure, get those quarterly sales figures and ask why they're not higher or commend the publisher if they are doing well. But do not fixate. Start writing something else at once. Put your attention elsewhere. Perhaps onto that new project that was flashing it shoulder at you when you're trying to complete the last one. Get fascinated. Fall in love all over again. By following this advice you will save yourself a great deal of mental effort worrying over every little fluctuation in your sales or bartering every tiny marketing point with your publisher. That's not why you got into writing, is it?

I assume you wanted to write because you wanted to create. Because you wanted to tell stories and bring people joy and connect with readers around the world, on the page. In the way only you can. So get on and do that. What's come before cannot be changed. Today is all you have. So make the most of it: write, craft and edit until you've got something you can be proud to put your name to: a story that could only have come from you.

GOOD WRITING DAY PROMPTS

The questions below relate to the topics explored in this book and offer a quick way of revising some of key elements I have discussed in the book. You do not have to go through the entire list every day. That would probably fall into the bracket of procrastination. You could just pick the most relevant question to your current circumstances and answer it in writing by timing yourself for ten minutes. The key thing is to be honest – this exploration is just for you. Nobody else is going to see it.

Are you firmly in the writer space? Have you quieted the editor? Are you ready to play and experiment on the page while nobody else is looking?

Are you focused on doing your best today without worrying what happened yesterday or what might happen tomorrow?

What is your purpose and why have you selected it?

Are you struggling to say what you want to with this piece? What are you trying to say? Would it help if you fictionalised the piece more heavily so that people didn't read an autobiographical quality into it? If you are writing non-fiction, why are you struggling to tell this story? What are your fears? What will people gain from you telling this story?

Are other tasks getting in the way of your writing time? How could you use them as writing material? Consider: plot, setting, characterisation and theme.

What other stories or poems are already published that resemble this piece of work? What do those pieces have in common? With this in mind, how could you surprise the reader by twisting one of these expected elements?

Are you unsure if this piece is finished? Does it fulfil your purpose? Does it convey the message you hoped? How will readers feel when they've finished reading it? Is that what you want? Is the transformation of your speaker or characters complete?

What kind of feedback have you received on this piece of writing so far? What do you like about it? What do you wish was better? How can you emphasise the strengths and minimise the flaws of this piece?

Have you received a rejection for this piece of writing? How did this make you feel? What action are you going to take to move forward from this setback?

Are you thinking of giving up on this project? Why? What will you gain if you give up on it? What will you lose?

Do you need to move on from your current project because you haven't found a publisher? What would you love to write next? What excites you about it? How might it excite readers? Why would writing this make you happy?

ACKNOWLEDGEMENTS

Heartfelt thanks to Dean Cummings and Ann Leander for the time they took to offer me feedback on this book. I do hope I handled your comments gracefully.

Thank you also to Hammad Khalid for his sparkling design skills and to my friends and family who have seen me through my many storms.

More Free Resources

If you would like a free creative writing starter library, including a publishing masterplan, 100 poetry prompts, a world-building masterplan and a character creation masterplan, please visit: helencoxbooks.com/creativewriters.

About the Author

Helen Cox is a Yorkshire-born novelist and poet. After completing her MA in creative writing at the University of York St. John Helen wrote for a range of magazines and websites as well as writing news and features for TV and radio. Helen edited her own independent film magazine for five years and has penned several non-fiction books. Her first two novels were published by HarperCollins in 2016. She currently hosts The Poetrygram podcast and coordinates poetry and non-fiction courses at City Lit, London. Helen's new series of cosy mysteries stars librarian-turned-sleuth Kitt Hartley, and is set in Yorkshire.

ALSO BY HELEN COX

How & When to Sign a Book Deal
How to Write Page-Turning Fiction
How to Write Sex
How & When to Quit Your Day Job

www.ingramcontent.com/pod-product-compliance
Lightning Source LLC
Chambersburg PA
CBHW071527080526
44588CB00011B/1578